CONVERGENCE

The Spirit-Led Journey

JOHN PHILLIP MOORE

WESTBOW
P R E S S®
A DIVISION OF THOMAS NELSON
& ZONDERVAN

All Scripture quotations, unless otherwise indicated, are taken from the Holy Bible, New International Version®, NIV®. Copyright ©1973, 1978, 1984, 2011 by Biblica, Inc.™ Used by permission of Zondervan. All rights reserved worldwide. www.zondervan.com The "NIV" and "New International Version" are trademarks registered in the United States Patent and Trademark Office by Biblica, Inc.™

Scripture taken from the King James Version of the Bible.

Scripture quotations are from the ESV® Bible (The Holy Bible, English Standard Version®), copyright © 2001 by Crossway, a publishing ministry of Good News Publishers. Used by permission. All rights reserved.

WestBow Press books may be ordered through booksellers or by contacting:

WestBow Press
A Division of Thomas Nelson & Zondervan
1663 Liberty Drive
Bloomington, IN 47403
www.westbowpress.com
1 (866) 928-1240

ISBN: 978-1-9736-5591-6 (sc)
ISBN: 978-1-9736-5592-3 (hc)
ISBN: 978-1-9736-5590-9 (e)

Library of Congress Control Number: 2019902797

Print information available on the last page.

WestBow Press rev. date: 03/25/2019

FOREWORD

"Convergence"...the word best describes how John Moore loves living life. John's life has been one unique assignment after another, all of them "converging" together to play out God's plan. This is a great read! You'll relate to it, learn from it and be challenged to live it out.

Mark Evans

INTRODUCTION

I live a life that is far from ordinary. I was raised in the wild land of Papua New Guinea (PNG), educated in Australia, and have lived many years in the United States of America. Currently, I'm living in Queensland, Australia. I surf, paint seascapes, and make great coffee for the neighborhood. My ministry includes extensive youth work, church planting, pastoring, leadership training, and crusading in Africa and India. God took ordinary me and placed his extraordinary fire within my soul. I'm very fortunate. God has blessed me with a wonderful family and deep moments with him that have radically redefined who I am and how I go about processing life. The Bible is my comfort, strength, and insight. That insight has created in me a fervor to know the Holy Spirit and to learn how he brings about the life that Jesus Christ talks about. I am writing from a Christian perspective, but my desire is that even if you are not sure what to believe, you will benefit from what I present.

I know you want to live out the best possible life that you can. In different ways, God has always been interested in you. I would care to guess that you haven't often taken the time to identify specific moments when God moved in you, through you, with you, and for you. My book will consider twelve specific observations. Each of the principles that I present will be illustrated through stories, and in turn they will become the anecdotal stimulation you need to interpret much more meaning for your own life. Each chapter is self-contained; systematic progress through the chapters is not necessary. You can read any section you like at any time, but I have strategically placed the chapters so that you don't miss out on certain considerations along the way. I want you to interpret your own journey through what you read and then take the time to reflect on areas that God will draw to your attention.

Life is never stagnant; you are going somewhere all the time. My desire is that, through convergence, you will grow closer to living your best possible Spirit-led journey.

Chapter 1

Calling

My beautiful wife, Cami, jumped up early on her birthday to go and see the phenomenon of the moon. It was an eclipse resulting in an extremely orange moon. I'm sure lots of people were doing the same. I missed it, but I've been fortunate to see similar displays while working in India. It's cool to be able to marvel at some of the unique ways that God sheds light on Earth.

Several years ago, when Cami was working as a travel agent in Los Angeles, she sent a large group of people from the Griffith Observatory to Greenland. Their quest was to see the northern lights, the spectacular light displays also known as the aurora borealis. It occurs in both hemispheres, but quite often it is ultramagnificent closest to the polar caps. While the technical aspects are varied, commonly, on the dark side of the Earth, particles from the sun collide with atoms in the Earth's atmosphere resulting in a breathtaking light show. It's the night side of the Earth that experiences a convergence of particles. These particles from the sun hit atoms in the Earth's atmosphere and charge electrons. The electrons are dispersed in some fashion. It's like the Earth announces its grandeur with a wild spray of light of intense color.

You must travel to specific locations to see how good the display is. The atmospheric conditions have to be favorable. Some people journey to these remote regions and miss what they long to see. You should arrive at the right time. If you are fortunate, you will see a light show beyond your wildest dreams through the convergence of what God brings into being.

This book is a Spirit-led journey that consists of twelve aspects of convergence. People are spiritual beings; in other words, there is a spiritual essence in being fully human. If we consider the bigger picture of life, it is that we journey through experiences and need to know there are some aspects that totally captivate us. There is no way that this book can cover everything about life, but I can be like a travel agent and direct you toward beautiful scenes that you need to see or at the very least reflect upon. It's in special moments that you can view the glory of God in his splendor.

Each chapter describes specific observations, each like a stream of thought that brings meaning and purpose into focus. When you consider the overall narrative of your life, imagine multiple streams flowing together to create a scenic river. There would be a whole lot more than twelve to consider, but the ones I have chosen will create a picture in the overall scheme of things.

Paul, the apostle of Jesus Christ, wrote, "We know that in all things God works together for the good of those who love him, and who have been called according to his purpose" (Romans 8:28). This is a foundational verse in all that I'm considering. It's a familiar scripture, but what it is saying is deeply majestic.

In life, you will have gone through experiences that you could have done without. And you may feel that you missed out on some aspects of life when other experiences did not manifest in your life. We've all had problems in our lives. Some things have upset us, and other things have spurred us on. Somehow, God is using all of this to draw us in to a journey that progresses throughout our lives. Through a guided reflective tour, you will see a clearer display of God's majestic will for your life. We all have a great deal of complexity in our stories, but it is fantastic to understand what happened to us wasn't a mistake but aspects of convergence.

The first stream that I will consider is *calling*. You have a calling on your life. This is ultimately important. You are not a random particle floating through some sort of meaningless existence. Your life's plan and purpose are worked out.

I think we naturally gravitate toward a self-determined life. Whatever we try to build or bring together, we do so to make a name for ourselves or eke out some sort of satisfaction. Sometimes, we want to be significant in doing so. We want good outcomes. So, when it comes to the spiritual side of our lives, there is a way that God brings something good into our lives. This is not about us being in control. Much like the particles of the sun that bring change to electrons in the darkness, God brings his spectacular light into the dark areas of our lives.

Recently, my wife and I traveled to North Stradbroke Island near Brisbane in Queensland, Australia. It is a beautiful place. We went over to the Pacific side of the island and stayed near the northern end. Right around the beaches are outcroppings of cliffs. The path we took wrapped around the top of the cliffs, and from there, we enjoyed the breathtaking tranquility of an amazing view.

There were different groups of people edging their way forward to sightsee. It was a bit of an adventurous experience. One family consisted of parents and two children. One was a boy who was around two years of age, and the other was a daughter who was around six. The six-year-old accompanied her father rather bravely to take in the view. The mother was not about to let the young boy do the same. For obvious reasons, the mother felt that the experience would be too risky for their rather rambunctious child. He was unimpressed by her caution. As far as he was concerned, his mother was withholding his freedom. The fact that his mother was protecting her son from injury or even death didn't enter his young head. He knew best. He ended up throwing a tantrum to protest his mother's unfair parenting practices. The little boy was quite cranky, and he defiantly told his mother, "No!" He wasn't going to stay with her. He was going with the other two.

The mother was frantic. "No, no! You can't go down there!" she said.

The little boy had no idea of the consequences he might endure. None! The mother knew her little boy. She knew what he was like. He had no idea what rested at the bottom of a fall. The mother was trying to protect her son.

Much like the little boy, we all have times in our lives when we believe we know what's best. It's like an innate ability. We base this "knowing" on a variety of experiences. I live with the thought that I know what is best for my life. I know what is important for me. Because I'm self-determined, I know how to make things happen. It's part of human nature.

Where does this come from?

The best way to grasp the complexity of these characteristics is to look at Adam and Eve. Their narrative makes a whole lot of sense. They—like us—were made in the image of God. Satan suggested they could ignore what God said and do what they wanted to do, and by doing so, they would be like God. That, my friends, seems to me to be a major part of our problems. The idea was presented to Eve. She didn't take much convincing.

4

Neither did Adam. The problem person was Adam. God had a package deal with Adam: enjoy everything, protect creation, and work well with Eve. There was only one rule: don't eat that particular fruit. But they ate what they should never have eaten. They went against God's specific instruction. It was a disastrous decision. Instantly, their perfect scenario was lost when they disobeyed God.

We have inherited the same predisposition that was illustrated in this story, which is often called "the fall." Whenever we are told we can't do something, we are drawn to do it. It is as if the forbidden presents a problem destined to be solved. But we need to remember that God has given us an extraordinary life of goodness as well. It's the same with kids. If you say to children, "You can have all this stuff, but you can't have that," guess what they want? Kids instantly want the forbidden thing. "I want that!" "I want to go there!" It's like a force within us.

Adam and Eve destroyed the beauty that existed in perfect paradise because they believed the wrong person. God is unlike his nemesis. God created us. God is holy. He doesn't sin. He is perfect. They had known only a perfect, unspoiled life: No guilt. No shame. No remorse. No disappointment. Everything changed for them. Their eyes were opened to see things that they had never seen before. They resolved to cover up what they could in their own way so that life seemed to make sense to them. For instance, prior to that fateful moment, they were happy being naked. But, instantly, they were concerned with their appearance. They tried to rectify the problem by making leaf coverings for their bodies.

We learn that the man and his wife heard God as he was walking in the garden, and they hid from God in the bushes because they were embarrassed and ashamed. God called to the man, "Where are you?" (Genesis 3:9).

Let's bring this back to our story. We do the same. We make up our own minds about how we are going to live, and our sin certainly causes us to avoid dealing with God. We hide from him. We are masters of delaying the inevitable. God comes looking for us in a spiritual sense. He calls to us in his way. If we are honest, the sin in our lives is embarrassing. Oh, we may have plenty of company in our sin. We can deny all sorts of things and validate our behaviors. But there is no way that we can meet with God without God doing something about the mess we are in. We may have created the drama or might be just caught up in it. You will appreciate that this is the calling that I'm talking about. If we see the basis of the principle, we see that God reaches out to us. He knows us. He is interested in us.

Refer to the Tower of Babel story in Genesis 11. People were told to go out and occupy the Earth and make children. They didn't want to do exactly as they were told. They wanted to do whatever they wanted to do, and they chose to stay put and build whatever they wanted to. They were determined to make a name for themselves and be the masters of their own lives. We learn that God himself changed their languages so that people could no longer understand each other. The resulting confused environment forced people to separate all over the world.

When you are trying to understand what is going on in your life and the lives of your family members and your friends, you need to be able to see more than your own circumstances. God doesn't leave himself out of what he has created. God is interested in people. God comes into the confusion that exists for one reason or another. God comes into what we are creating; it is his way of getting our attention.

I've met so many people, and I've seen how they are wandering through life. We often want to solve problems by giving advice. Somehow, we want to take away the reality of what is really going on. God is still the one in his way who "walks" into any situation in any environment and says, "Where are you?" You will hear his silent voice. These are spiritual moments between God and yourself. Your greatest problems stem from a spiritual dilemma. When God gets close to us, God is trying to bring about a change in us. When God is moving into this environment, he is moving in on our lives.

The normal patterns of people's lives often fall apart as they experience problems with people in their jobs, families, schools, and circle of friends. They start asking, "Why is this happening?" They expect everything to be better than it is. "Why are the kids disobedient?" "Why did I not get that grade?" "Why is everything mixed up?" When these things are fully raging, you can be sure that God is asking, "Where are you?"

We may have a greater mindfulness that things aren't right. When we see someone going through a difficult time, we want to give him or her our best and most practical advice. You hear people say, "When I went through that problem ...," and then they share what they learned from others, from books, or from some other experience. The great work of God is us. He is more concerned with all of us than any of us will be concerned about others around us.

In our own way, we avoid God. There is something within our will that prefers to go against what is right and true. We have a sinful nature. It's real. Essentially, it's a disease with a death sentence. We may hide this part of our lives. If we are confronted with our own wrongdoing, we try to avoid the truth (maybe because of consequences), but we still desire to win the approval of others. Most people want to look good.

Some people give up with the whole masquerade of being good, and they flaunt their rebellion and wickedness as a cool way of life.

Adam and Eve ran away. They hid. God asked them who they had been listening to. (They had been listening to the wrong voice.) Who have you been listening to? Who told you that you are the way that you are? Adam blamed God and Eve. Eve blamed Satan. We do the same. When something goes wrong, we get embarrassed and go into default mode by blaming someone. Our sin problem is a spiritual one. God by his Spirit works in our lives to fix what is messed up.

Go all the way to the person of Jesus Christ. Jesus, the son of God, came to Earth as a baby. You only have to picture the angels and stars announcing his arrival. It was a converge of the spectacular. God, who is Spirit, sent his son as one of us. Jesus didn't come as a spirit. Jesus came as a real human child. The difference between Jesus and every other human being is that he never sinned. He remained innocent. Perfect.

As a grown man, Jesus gathered people. He was constantly drawing people to himself. They were called his disciples or followers, and they became his friends. There were groups of other people who didn't like Jesus. Indeed, they felt threatened by his presence. Some people hated him. Those people had him falsely arrested, tried, convicted, and condemned to death. The Romans embraced the whole concept of crucifixion by nailing or binding a criminal to a large wooden cross as the cruelest method of torturing a person to death. Jesus was falsely accused of a crime. He went through an unjust trial, and he was sentenced to die on a cross. He was beaten severely and made to carry a heavy wooden cross out of the city of Jerusalem to the execution site. He was crucified on a Roman cross until he died. His death was intentional. God sent his son, Jesus, to die for the sins of the whole world. It wasn't an accident or a mistake. It was planned. God knew how sinful humankind would respond to his perfect son. Then Jesus was resurrected from death three days later. His resurrection is proof that whatever work was done on the cross was God's perfect plan. God raised him back to life. The sin problem that Adam created for all humankind was solved at the cross by Christ's sacrifice, and it was confirmed in the resurrection.

Jesus wasn't simply planning to build a group of fanatical religious followers. He wasn't starting a religion. He built his church. He offered hope to people all over the world. Humanity, for all its wonder, is in a hopeless spiritual predicament. Jesus loves us. He established how God would call people into a right relationship established through forgiveness of sins on that cross. He intended to send his friends into the world with that wonderful message of grace and goodness. We get a chance to start life all over again when we accept this message. The light of the world—Jesus—sent himself out with his disciples. There is a "light display" on planet Earth called the church. Jesus was under orders from God to do what he was asked to do—and he did it.

> Then the eleven disciples went to Galilee, to the mountain where Jesus had told them to go. When they saw him, they worshipped him; but some doubted. Then Jesus came to them and said, "All authority in heaven and on earth has been given to me. Therefore, go and make disciples of all nations, baptizing them in the name of the Father and of the Son and of the Holy Spirit, and teaching them to obey everything I have commanded you. And surely,

I am with you always, to the very end of the age."
(Matthew 28:16–20)

The disciples worshipped him, but even as they did, some were uncertain about who he was. Jesus had been given all authority to act on Earth in accordance with God's plan for humankind. In this we see a charge. It wasn't a suggestion. Jesus called the disciples to himself. He had the authority to do so. It wasn't simply a request to make Jewish people into followers of Jesus Christ; it was a commission to people to reach out to more people of every ethnic origin on Earth. Every people group on planet Earth was included.

An interesting part of the calling is one of teaching obedience in everything he commanded. People are more likely to do what they want to do. What was Jesus thinking about? What did he command? What was different? This goes all the way back to the beginning. When God commanded Adam not to eat the fruit in the middle of the garden, he expected obedience.

God commanded Adam not to eat a specific fruit, and Jesus told his disciples to teach people about the importance of obeying all his commands. There is a huge difference. Jesus intended to be with his "friends." He was in them. However, we know he wasn't going to be physically with them.

Churches today know we are under the dual charge of the great "love" command and the great "outreach" commission, but when you consider the complexity of what Jesus is asking, you should know we need help; otherwise, we just don't do it. It doesn't happen.

Remember the Northern Lights, the spectacular display in the sky? You must go to where it displays if you want to see it. We can learn all about the facts of how particles charge the electrons and how gases are involved to stimulate a wonderful phenomenon. I'm not a scientist. I have no idea what is really taking place. I'm just happy to say, "Look at that!"

When we try to understand the ways of God, we should consider more than just facts. The ways of God are factual and spiritual! You experience a sort of convergence happening in you. It's not something you do to yourself. This is what God does. In fact, God does something to you that you can't conceivably do to yourself. We are called to God the Father through God the Son in the power of God the Holy Spirit. We have a choice in how we respond.

A religious group leader called Nicodemus came to Jesus at night. He didn't want his compatriots to think he had gone over to the other side. I think he wanted to get the best out of his life, and he knew it wasn't happening. He didn't know if he could associate with Jesus or not. He came on the dark side of night. He went into a deep and meaningful conversation with Jesus.

> Jesus replied, "Very truly I tell you, no one can see the kingdom of God unless they are born again."
>
> "How can someone be born when they are old?" Nicodemus asked.
>
> "Surely they cannot enter a second time into their mother's womb to be born!"
>
> Jesus answered, "Very truly I tell you, no one can enter the kingdom of God unless they are born of water and the Spirit. Flesh gives birth to flesh, but the Spirit gives birth to spirit. You should not be surprised at my saying, 'You must

be born again.' The wind blows wherever it pleases. You hear its sound, but you cannot tell where it comes from or where it is going. So it is with everyone born of the Spirit."

"How can this be?" Nicodemus asked. (John 3:3–9)

Jesus was talking about a change in someone's life that would cause the person to be no longer empowered by self-determinism. In fact, God would come in and change everything. Jesus explained how things come together or why we might miss out completely:

> For God so loved the world that he gave his one and only Son, that whoever believes in him shall not perish but have eternal life. For God did not send his Son into the world to condemn the world, but to save the world through him. Whoever believes in him is not condemned, but whoever does not believe stands condemned already because they have not believed in the name of God's one and only Son. This is the verdict: light has come into the world, but people loved darkness instead of light because their deeds were evil. Everyone who does evil hates the light, and will not come into the light for fear that their deeds will be exposed. But whoever lives by the truth comes into the light, so that it may be seen plainly that what they have done has been done in the sight of God. (John 3:16–21)

There is no possible way that we can really grasp how much God loves the world. We just learn that "God so loved the world" (John 3:16). We see in scripture that we need to recognize him for who he is, and that he calls us for our own good.

Why is there so much confusion in families? People say they have so much stress in their lives, and they ask, "Where is God?" People feel that God is not part of their lives when, in fact, he is present through every movement of life. We are trying to process all sorts of experiences and emotions without God's input. Scripture says that people loved darkness. Self-determinism has its root in us as we try to go our own way. If you ever hear God calling you to come, you want to give parts of your life to God but not all, not your whole life, because you fear that you will lose something significant. It means a radical change in your life. We ask ourselves questions: What do you mean, I'm not the boss of my life, the master of my own destiny? What do you mean I have to give this up? To whom?

You see? That's the extraordinary call of the gospel. The gospel message is a calling.

The way I see it, the cross of Christ stands as God's promise of extraordinary love. There is not a person on the planet who has been right with God because of their goodness. It's not because of your religious heritage. It's not because you go to church. It's by the cross of Jesus Christ. God sent his son to Earth to die on the cross to pay for your sin and for my sin: Sin. Is. Paid. In. Full. That is the good news of the gospel. That is the work of the cross. There is a spectacular convergence of light shed on your life because of the blood shed on the cross. It's done. It's finished. Christ died for you and for me. Your sin requires death as punishment. Jesus offers a complete pardon so you can live. The cross of Jesus is our claimable access to God and his kingdom.

Even today, is God calling you? You might be saying that you don't know what is wrong in your life. Maybe you feel that you have tried to explain things to yourself. Is he calling you to himself? Tell God today that you are listening, and you require his forgiveness because you have sinned against him. We all have.

You may have questions about many things. You may be connected to what I'm saying but unsure of what it means to you. The good thing about what I'm writing is that it is spiritual in nature. You can converse with God by simply talking to him or praying to him. Talk to Jesus right now. Tell him you believe who he is, what he has done. Tell him you want to follow him with your life.

CHAPTER 2

SACRIFICE

Your life is dynamic; it's always changing. When we consider the Spirit-led journey, we know that we are going somewhere. It's not a fixed situation. There are variables. And with the convergence of various factors creating movement and flow in your life, we examine the Spirit's influence and our interaction. Nothing is stagnant. We may have routines, but what happens when God changes your life?

I think that, far too often, we underrate the Christian experience of life. It's as if somewhere, somehow you become a Christian, and then you get into a church to grow. But how? We develop all sorts of programs that are rooted with some sort of intentionality, but the Spirit isn't managed by one of our programs. He moves only the way he chooses to move. The challenge is moving with him in some meaningful rhythm and flow of love.

God calls you to journey with him. You have a calling. What is often overlooked is that we will encounter the principle of sacrifice along the way.

As I have mentioned, I was raised in Papua New Guinea (PNG), an island nation just north of Australia. My parents were originally employed on a mission station in the valley of the Baiyer River in the western highlands. This is a beautiful, picturesque place. A gravel road winds its way through the valley. My dad used to drive way too fast. I loved his enthusiastic driving skills. Dad could slide his Toyota Land Cruiser through every corner flat out as fast as possible. I was shaped by my father. I grew up totally enthralled with cars and with a love of driving fast on gravel roads. I was aware of the sport of rally driving, and I was blessed with a good deal of imagination. I developed an aspiration to race.

As a young man, I got my turn to grow up and get my license and own cars. We continued to live in PNG, and I not only was interested in driving way too fast on gravel roads, I became aware that I had a good deal of natural, God-given talent for racing cars. I could drive fast, and I never crashed.

Eventually, I moved from PNG to the United States of America. While I was living in Arkansas, I saw a segment on the local news about rally racing in the northern part of the state. Instantly, I became super interested and looked into the sport. I quickly connected with the right people and began racing. My business in sign manufacturing was going rather well, finances were good, and so I managed to get involved with a racing series that traveled to various states in America. I would venture off to all sorts of remote forest regions and have a great time.

On one occasion, I was in Ohio with my support crew. My co-driver was Mike. Mike was a terrific mechanic, but he was probably not the best navigator (and he would agree with me!). The navigator aids the driver by following instructions and diagrams in a book specifically made for each race. We had raced throughout the day with all sorts of drama and hiccups. It wasn't a great event for us. However, one of the last segments or stages of the race happened late at night—around

11:30 pm. We were charging as hard as possible to make up for lost time. We were in a Mazda RX7, which was very light and super quick. The road was through the Chillicothe Forest. We were going downhill, and I had my accelerator pedal flat to the floor. Rally cars are fitted with extraordinary lights that illuminate the road brilliantly. Mike was supposed to be giving me instructions, but he was unusually quiet. I asked him an important question: "What's the call?" Co-drivers call out each corner in advance via the aid of a computer of sorts. Mike yelled over the intercom, "Straight on. Flat out!" Those words still ring out in my memory. Everything was extremely loud. Rocks were smashing against the under carriage. We were traveling close to 150 miles per hour on a road we had never seen before.

Something within me told me that Mike was dead wrong. I slammed on the brakes. The Mazda had huge brakes that acted like anchors. I smashed down through the gears and barely made it through a ninety-degree right-hand corner. It was actually a T-intersection. There was no "road" ahead of us. There was only a track with orange barricade tape draped across it.

Mike was instantly apologetic. "I'm sorry! So sorry!" he blurted out. He tried to explain his mistake. He was on the wrong page. He had become mesmerized by the speed at which we were traveling. I was silent. I wasn't mad. I just knew something huge had moved us through that moment. We got back to the staging area where all the cars assembled, and Mike went off to check on our race times. When he got back, he was visibly shaken and extremely upset. It turns out that, if we had charged through the barricade tape and continued, we would have launched ourselves into certain death. There was a canyon beyond that intersection.

I felt as if I'd had a huge moment that night with God himself. Yes, he had steered us using some sort of guidance. But also, I became aware that, at that critical moment, I had become extremely "me" centered in life. I knelt beside the car, and I prayed to God. It was a starry night, and the air was crisp. I promised God that I would get out of racing and devote my life to whatever he had in mind. It wasn't that it felt wrong to race; rather, I felt that God was offering me something beyond what I had, but I had to be willing to give something up—something that I loved to do. I raced once more, in Paris, Texas, that year, and then sold everything up. With a desire to serve God in some sort of capacity, I headed to Australia.

Some people are super talented and awesome at everything they do, but that's not me. I'm ordinary. When I discovered I was quite good at racing cars on gravel roads, I felt I had found meaning and purpose to my life. God, in his calling for my life, had something else in mind. It seems to me that God will allow us to keep doing what we want to do in life, or what we think is important, and then we develop a willingness to sacrifice. This is personal. Your story is not my story. You will have your own moments with God that change your destiny or realign your focus toward what is important to him.

In Genesis we learn that Abraham lived with a sense of purpose knowing that God was going to bless the whole world through his life. Talk about a meaningful existence! God promised Abraham that he was going give him a massive family starting with his son Isaac. The problem was that God tested the faith of Abraham in a story that goes completely outside our realm of thinking. Abraham and Sarah couldn't have children for a long time, and then Isaac was born. They had waited twenty-five years to have him. A huge story unfolded in their lives when God told Abraham to go and sacrifice his son: "Then God said, 'Take your son, your only son, whom you love—Isaac—and go to the region of Moriah. Sacrifice him there as a burnt offering on a mountain that I will show you'" (Genesis 22:2).

Abraham's story takes place 1,800 years or so before Jesus's life here on Earth. This story is monumental and has connections all the way through to Jesus and the cross. Abraham and Isaac traveled to the exact location on which Jerusalem was built. Nothing existed at that time. Everything was constructed later. God told Abraham to take his son as a sacrifice. Remember, it had taken twenty-five years of waiting before Isaac was born, and then God told Abraham to kill him. Interestingly, Abraham didn't know where the mountain was, but God promised to reveal the location as Abraham traveled with Isaac. Understand the faith of Abraham. He knew God had promised Isaac as his son to fulfil the rest of God's promises. By the way, Abraham didn't run the plan by his wife Sarah.

> Early the next morning Abraham got up and loaded his donkey. He took with him two of his servants and his son Isaac. When he had cut enough wood for the burnt offering, he set out for the place God had told him about. On the third day Abraham looked up and saw the place in the distance. He said to his servants, "Stay here with the donkey while I and the boy go over there. We will worship and then we will come back to you." (Genesis 22:3–5)

There are four humans involved in this story—two servants, Abraham, and Isaac. You will notice that Abraham told the servants to wait where they were. He told them that he and Isaac would both return after their time of worship. He fully intended to do two things. He intended to kill Isaac, and he intended to return with Isaac, but not just with a dead body. No, there was going to be fire involved. He was going to burn the body of Isaac. And yet he also intended bringing back a very-much alive Isaac. He believed God could raise his son from the dead. He knew that Isaac was part of the picture for their family's future. This is an extraordinary story of faith. Abraham assured the servants that they would be coming back.

> Abraham took the wood for the burnt offering and placed it on his son Isaac, and he himself carried the fire and the knife. As the two of them went on together, Isaac spoke up and said to his father Abraham, "Father?"
>
> "Yes, my son?" Abraham replied.
>
> "The fire and wood are here," Isaac said, "but where is the lamb for the burnt offering?"
>
> Abraham answered, "God himself will provide the lamb for the burnt offering, my son." And the two of them went on together. (Genesis 22:6–8)

Do you see the picture of Jesus paralleled in this story? The wood is placed on the son and carried to the actual site of sacrifice—the same site that Jesus went to. Abraham believed his son was the lamb for the sacrifice.

> When they reached the place God had told him about, Abraham built an altar there and arranged the wood on it. He bound his son Isaac and laid him on the altar, on top of the wood.

> Then he reached out his hand and took the knife
> to slay his son. But the angel of the Lord called
> out to him from heaven, "Abraham! Abraham!"
>
> "Here I am," he replied.
>
> "Do not lay a hand on the boy," he said. "Do not
> do anything to him. Now I know that you fear
> God, because you have not withheld from me
> your son, your only son." (Genesis 22:9-12)

Isaac was silent, much like Jesus was silent. Innocent. Talk about a last-second reprieve.

> Abraham looked up and there in a thicket he
> saw a ram caught by its horns. He went over
> and took the ram and sacrificed it as a burnt
> offering instead of his son. So Abraham called
> that place The Lord Will Provide. And to this
> day it is said, "On the mountain of the Lord it
> will be provided." (Genesis 22:13,14)

The ram was provided, crowned in thorns, much as there was an innocent one provided for the sins of the world in Jesus. Abraham had to wait so long in his life for promises of God to come to fruition. In fact, he never lived in the land knowing that he owned the land. That part of the story came much later.

James, in the New Testament, wrote about what Abraham did and how that story becomes an example for people living out their faith.

> Was not our father Abraham considered
> righteous for what he did when he offered his

son Isaac on the altar? You see that his faith
and his actions were working together, and his
faith was made complete by what he did. And
the scripture was fulfilled that says, "Abraham
believed God, and it was credited to him as
righteousness," and he was called God's friend.
You see that a person is considered righteous
by what they do and not by faith alone. (James
2:21–24)

Sacrificing children in pagan settings was common. It's a
bizarre story to become so central in the message about living
out your life. It almost seems like an awful encounter with God.
Many people have deep questions about how God could suggest
such a sacrifice or how he could put Abraham through such an
ordeal and call it a test. It all comes down to righteousness.
This is the central tenant in Jewish theology concerning one's
right standing with God. James is reminding his readers that
not only was Abraham considered "right" with God, because
of the way he interacted with God, he was considered God's
friend. What a great relationship he had, to be considered
the friend of God. In what I'm presenting in this book, this is
the outworking of your faith—friendship with God. "Faith"
that doesn't result in action isn't faith; it is a dead end. True
faith is part of life in this, our journey with God. It takes us
somewhere. It must. It is important for us to know that we
are justified by faith. The basis of our relationship with God is
based on a declaration that we are right with God because of
Jesus Christ. The outworking of your life is the happenings of
your faith through a convergence with Christ.

In Mark's gospel, Jesus puts your purpose in life into perspective:

> Then he called the crowd to him along with his disciples and said: "Whoever wants to be my disciple must deny themselves and take up their cross and follow me. For whoever wants to save their life will lose it, but whoever loses their life for me and for the gospel will save it. What good is it for someone to gain the whole world, yet forfeit their soul? Or what can anyone give in exchange for their soul?" (Mark 8:34–37)

Abraham had specific moments with God. One time he was called outside to see the vision God had for his life. Whether a dream or a vision, Abraham received a picture of all the stars shining in the universe. It was in that moment that he was declared righteous. God basically said to him that, as numerous as the countless stars in the heavens were, so his offspring would be. Abraham didn't question God. He believed God and, in that moment, was declared righteous. When God told Abraham to sacrifice his son, Abraham prepared to do it. That is faith lived out.

In the story of Jesus, we read that Jesus painted a picture of each of those who became his disciples. We have bought into what he was talking about. We embark on a journey, carrying our crosses as we follow behind Jesus. There are things in our lives that we think are important, but we are tested in different ways. God has action in mind for our lives. Jesus knew that he had the cross to carry so that he could bear the sins of the world. In your life, as in the story of Peter, when Jesus asked him, "Do you love me more than these [fish]?" (John 21:15), you will have an opportunity to live out God's plans for your life.

Now this does not necessarily mean a change in occupation, but there will be different requirements in your journey that is led by the Spirit.

We are his disciples. We are tested in unique ways. Sacrifice happens. We learn when to lay down something and when to pick up what he has in mind for us to do. I look back on racing in my life. Perhaps it had become an idol in my life; I don't know for sure. It certainly took a great deal of time, energy, and focus. Maybe it wasn't my idol. It's easy for people to look at my life and tell me I shouldn't have been doing that because it was a foolhardy endeavor. But that is my story. You have your story. There will be times in your life when you encounter God, and he will tell you that he wants you to do something different with your life. Scripture says for you to offer yourself as a living sacrifice—*living.* Jesus commissions your life.

You can pursue a multitude of interests in your life, but you will miss out on the best that he has for you. What's the point of losing yourself in something that doesn't really amount to anything? Can you hear what he is asking you to do? We have choices to make.

These are hard principles to get your head around. It's about sacrificing to God something that is precious to you. Sometimes we want to hang on to what we think is important. We want to hang on to our jobs, our money, our kids, our possessions. But we get a nudge from God to move somewhere. I don't mean a geographic move; rather, I mean relational move closer to the Spirit, under his influence. Certainly, moving to another country is hard—pack up your belongings and go here or there. Or better yet, get rid of everything you have and move somewhere you have never been. It's hard. We are so used to being comfortable that we don't go anywhere. Our routines are unchangeable. God will unsettle you when he decides to unsettle you. He will call you to wherever he decides to call you. This is the extraordinary work in the gospel. We are to be like Abraham and obey. This is part of our lives. This is not easy. Don't think that giving away something that you treasure is easy. Take, for instance, a wife who has to walk away from an abusive marriage. This is a huge problem in our society. Our society views marriage highly. Instantly, there is remorse in a necessary choice. Marriage is not the most important institution on Earth. The most important relationship is with God. He calls you into what is right. You may think that something about you defines you. We put all sorts of things ahead of God—important things like marriage and family. But none of these is higher than your identity and your relationship with God.

You don't get to move on with God until you let go of what he calls you to let go of. In the story of Abraham, Abraham had no idea which mountain he was going to; he simply embarked upon a journey of progressive revelation. God said, "I will show you" (Genesis 22:2). That is often the case with God.

Trust me. I have always wanted to know all the details about everything: What do you mean? Where exactly am I going? Where is the financing coming from? How is this or that going to come together?

God tested Abraham to prove that Abraham believed God would provide for him. That was Abraham's faith: God would provide. He knew that Isaac was God's gift and that there was a reason for his existence. So it is with our lives. We have a faith journey to follow. Our existence is not a stagnant one. We are encouraged to join a Bible-believing church and grow in faith. You will grow through a variety of means, but sacrifice is essential in your life.

Jesus was represented completely through the story of Abraham and Isaac. He would come to planet Earth for you and for me. He knew what was on offer. He knew he was the sacrifice for sin. He realized he was not only God's son but that he was the lamb God provided. We also know that he forecast not only the wooden cross, but also his resurrection. He knew he was going to go through an awful and terrible ordeal. He took elements from the Passover meal to bring his disciples together for good. He took the bread to remind them of his body in the sacrifice. He also took the wine to remind them of his blood on the altar. However, it's in the resurrection of the dead that we have hope for the future. It's the ultimate convergence for his followers to believe in.

CHAPTER 3

SUBMISSION

When we are trying to understand the dynamic working of God in our lives, we shouldn't try to see the aspects that I'm touching on to be in some sort of sequential order. They are observations of a life lived out.

One of the most popular conversations that I have with people is introduced when they ask me, "Am I doing what God wants me to do with my life?" This is a niggling thought that many Christian people wrestle with. I think what drives us is the underlying thought that there must be some sort of assignment that God expects us to carry out, and we wonder if we are somehow neglecting our God-given responsibilities. This is common. It's also a healthy spiritual thought. While I'm not going to get into every aspect of God's will for your life, I would like to point out some things that I see.

In the Old Testament there is a great verse that I and many others have loved: "Trust in the Lord with all your heart and lean not on your own understanding, in all your ways submit to him and he will make your paths straight" (Proverbs 3:5–6).

I like the idea of trusting God with all my heart. And I know that my understanding has various flaws. The revelation for this concept is found in the word *submit*. Years ago, the New

27

International Version Bible translated this scripture differently. It used the word *acknowledge* rather than submit. Technically, *submit* is a far more accurate translation. However, I learned this verse using *acknowledge*. In some ways, I felt that, if we acknowledge God in our decision-making processes, things would work out the way God wants them to work out. The truth is that God intends to direct our paths, and submitting to him enables us to see the great choices he gives us. Submitting is a game changer for us.

I want to explain submission using an example of something that I don't do well—dancing. My wife, Cami, loves to dance, and she can dance beautifully. I'm not sure why, but dancing is never going to be my "thing." I'm talking about ballroom dancing here—a waltz or a tango. In these dances, two people must work together with amazing rhythm and purpose. In this type of dance, one person leads, and the other follows. While each may have his or her own variations in steps and movements, there is a definite pattern of harmony and a connection in the artform. Similarly, in our lives, the Holy Spirit leads, and we follow in the Spirit-led journey of life.

If you think about our salvation, you will realize that we needed Jesus Christ to save us. That's his great work. We cannot save ourselves; it's impossible. Salvation through Jesus is God's great gift to humanity. And, along that same line of thinking, we realize that we can't guide our salvation. This is the great work of the Spirit of God. It's not that we can somehow live our lives our way and add the Holy Spirit into our lives. No! We read in Galatians that we must keep in step with the Spirit (Galatians 5:25). He leads. Wherever he leads we follow. We get to work out our salvation, but we don't have to figure out our salvation by our own means. Now, we may not be very good at keeping up. We might even want to give up. Somehow, he keeps encouraging us to keep going.

When people ask if they are doing what God wants them to do with their lives, they are asking a healthy question. If we are not asking that sort of mind-derived question, we are probably walking alone.

In a dance, it is usually the man who leads and the woman willingly submits to that leadership. Gladly she follows. It's always God who leads us. This is the grace of God. His free-loving grace is poured out through love. There is a convergence in our lives when we gladly submit willingly to his leading. We might say, "Not my will, but yours." This becomes our hearts' desire. Submission helps us keep in step with what God is saying to us.

There is a great story about people trying to figure out their lives. It's in the Old Testament. Zechariah, a post-exilic prophet, writes about the Israelites' struggle to do the right thing. A brief history of Israel helps us to understand their hardships. During the reign of King David, peace was established. The king who succeeded him also experienced peace. However, idols and foreign religions crept into the mix. The nation divided into two segments—the northern tribes and the remaining southern tribes. Assyria annihilated the ten northern tribes. Later Babylonia captured the southern tribes and took people into exile. Thus, the exile is a major point in Bible history. Sometime after the exile, people who returned to Israel began to live with good intentions, but they went back to old ways that had existed before the exile. Technically, those ways had got the people into all the mess that resulted in the exile. People began to grumble. Grumbling is easy to do. It's a bit of a pattern in Israel. It had also happened right after the people came out of Egypt way back when Moses guided them.

This became a way of life for Israelites. In Zechariah's writings, the people were asking God what he wanted them to do.

> In the fourth year of King Darius, the word of the Lord came to Zechariah on the fourth day of the ninth month, the month of Kislev. The people of Bethel had sent Sharezer and Regem-Melek, together with their men, to entreat the Lord by asking the priests of the house of the Lord Almighty and the prophets, "Should I mourn and fast in the fifth month, as I have done for so many years?"
>
> Then the word of the Lord Almighty came to me: "Ask all the people of the land and the priests, "When you fasted and mourned in the fifth and seventh months for the past seventy years, was it really for me that you fasted? And when you were eating and drinking, were you not just feasting for yourselves? Are these not the words the Lord proclaimed through the earlier prophets when Jerusalem and its surrounding towns were at rest and prosperous, and the Negev and the western foothills were settled?"
>
> And the word of the Lord came again to Zechariah: "This is what the Lord Almighty said: 'Administer true justice; show mercy and compassion to one another. Do not oppress the widow or the fatherless, the foreigner or the poor. Do not plot evil against each other.'"

"But they refused to pay attention; stubbornly they turned their backs and covered their ears. They made their hearts as hard as flint and would not listen to the law or to the words that the Lord Almighty had sent by his Spirit through the earlier prophets. So, the Lord Almighty was very angry.

"'When I called, they did not listen; so, when they called, I would not listen,' says the Lord Almighty. 'I scattered them with a whirlwind among all the nations, where they were strangers. The land they left behind them was so desolate that no one travelled through it. This is how they made the pleasant land desolate.'"
(Zechariah 7:1–14)

They were asking an important question about when they should fast. God answered them by asking them a question in return about whom they were fasting for. It was a good question for them, and it's a good question for us. Really, for whom are we living? Why do we go to church? For them it was about fasting. Fasting is a religious practice, but why did they do this? He was seeing that the people were eating for their own reasons and living their lives for themselves. The people were supposed to be looking after the oppressed, the disadvantaged, the widows and orphans, and the newcomers to the land. However, historically, people had ignored God's request to help others. They simply ignored the social problems around them and focused on their own prosperity. They wanted God to bless them, so they performed religious practices to earn his favor. They got it mixed up.

The truth was that God had established the Mosaic laws to ensure that people were cared for, but the people of the Israelite nation ignored what was in scripture. God also sent his appointed prophets. Those men played a key role in the Old Testament; they were virtually the voice of God for the people. But history shows that the people often ignored the prophets. They even killed them because they didn't like what they said. By rejecting the word of God, the people hardened their hearts to what God was trying to do in their lives.

In the New Testament, Christian people are referred to as new creations. We get new hearts and new spirits. In the Old Testament, God wrote his rules in stone. In some sort of metaphorical way, God impresses upon our hearts his will for our lives. His written word in the Bible speaks to our souls. We have opportunities to listen to what he is saying and to believe his words. In like fashion, we can reject the message, but then our hearts will begin to harden against what God would like to teach us. God teaches us that our hearts are the wellsprings of our thoughts. If we get things muddled up, it's often because our hearts are confused. If we submit to the Lord, we learn that he guides our paths. His word illuminates our moves with him. While we are new creations, we learn that there is a shift in us. God operates the way he chooses to work in us, and we learn to cooperate with him.

Zechariah's message says that God was angry at the people. We don't like to think of God getting angry, but he does get angry. Too often we have some sort of picture of God as a teddy bear sort of character in the universe, or that he is like a vending machine that coughs up what we want if we pray correctly. He is not like a teddy bear. He is nothing like a vending machine. God has feelings. He can be hurt when he is rejected. You must understand that everything in creation begins with a thought in God's mind. The whole universe was created because God thought it up. God started with you in mind. You began first in the mind of God. God is far beyond feeble, broken humanity. God is worthy to be worshipped. He alone is awesome. The question addressed in this passage was why the people were fasting. Did they carry out their religious practices for the right reasons? Or were they doing it to satisfy some sort of tradition that they had created? We need to look at our own routines. Why do we go to church? Sometimes people go to church because that's what Christians do. You might have grown up in a church and never really thought about why you attended. Church might be your routine. The question we must answer is this: Why do we keep doing what we do?

We know that God is a God of love—supreme love. What we forget is that his anger is an expression of his total love for his creation. The passage says, "When I called, they did not listen; so when they called, I would not listen" (Zechariah 7:13). That scripture is not how I would think God would be. I don't picture God like this. But when the people ignored God, God stopped listening to what the people were saying. Understand that God is unchanging. He still works like this. The word was in scripture, and it was the prophet's very message, but the people rejected both areas of revelation.

God then told them that, in history, he had scattered the people. The land itself was out of vogue with God's favor, and it was obvious that the land was totally useless. When the Israelite people occupied the region, it was described as a land flowing with milk and honey. It was a very productive region; while they were in the exile, it was cursed, or at the very least, unable to experience his blessings. When the Israelites left Jerusalem, it was a mess, a barren wasteland.

In Australia, as I write, I can't help but think that we are in a drought for a variety of reasons. Largely, we are rejecting God and what he has said in his scriptures. We have been in a drought for quite some time. The farmers are in dire straits. The conditions are awful. It's affecting our whole country. It's the farmers who are being oppressed. How much of this is a result of God being sick and tired of us ignoring him? Sure, we can explain the science behind the drought, but can we grasp how the scientist writes the plot? The truth is that our nation is spiritually dry. It's not the first drought, and it's not the first time that we have ignored God. It's not the farmers' fault that it is not raining on the land. It is obvious that God isn't breaking the drought.

People in the cities are complaining about the rising cost of meat. I almost wish it would go up ten times, and then we would begin to grasp how tough it is to be a farmer, and we might grow an appreciation for how good our lives have been. Our lives are traditionally easy. Why? Because, primarily, this is a nation built upon the premise of God and his word. This fact is eroding, and we are starting to see how tough the future might become. The whole nation has gone through spiritual routines, but we, as a nation, have forgotten why we do what we do. We must ask ourselves: Why do we go to church? Why do we pray? Why do we read our Bibles? Why do we connect with some people and fellowship with others?

If we don't do these things as acts of worship to God, we are missing the point of why we exist. We have been given our lives, been given salvation, and we are to worship God with our lives. So, when we ask "What am I doing with my life?" we need to know that the answer is that our entire lives should be acts of worship to God. We exist to bring him the glory that is his. We all go through moments in which we want our assignments in life. We ask God, "What do you want me to do?" God has his word. He has spoken. It's a theme that runs through the whole Bible, from Genesis right through to Revelation. "Whoever has ears, let them hear what the Spirit says to the churches" (Revelation 3:13). This sums up God's desire. We need to listen with ears that want to absorb what he says.

This is what I think is important when we consider living out our lives. If we are not concerned about personal sin, more than likely we are not going anywhere. In this life, our spiritual journey is to follow the Holy Spirit. If we are not conscious of our own personal sin, we have a problem. If you are saying to yourself that you are a pretty good person and that you are doing all the right things with your life, I would really question whether you are in step with the Holy Spirit. I think that the person who is truly walking with God will have many opportunities to reflect on where he or she messed things up. If you are justifying your own righteousness, you soon become self-righteousness. If you are saying, "I didn't do so well with that" or "I feel that I'm inadequate in my life" or "My life doesn't really look the way it should," I think you are on the right path. If you are aware of your sin, that is a good thing. If you recognize God's ideals and your mediocre goodness, good! I recognize that, and I grumble. This does not happen only when I'm tired. I grumble just because I grumble. What about you? Do we share this trait? I don't have an excuse for it, and I can't justify it.

The problem is that, if I live grumbling and say that everything going wrong in our nation is everyone else's fault, I am in grave error. The truth is that I have a problem too—a spiritual problem—because I have let the Holy Spirit impress upon my heart that I'm grumbling.

Do you recognize that you don't have the patience that you should have? Do you recognize that you don't have the kindness that you should have or the love for people that you should have?

I believe you are not going anywhere if you think you are ticking all the "God boxes" in your life. You have camped out on your own and are unaware that God is no longer speaking to you. However, if you know you need help with your life, you, my friend, are on a journey with God himself. You might worry about too many things. You might not be doing so well with your marriage, your family, or your job. These are your moments for God to impress upon your heart his way for you. You need to seize these moments and be ready to listen to him. Your realization of the "messed-up-ness" in your life is not a bad thing. No. In fact, it's a good thing. You might say, John, where do you get those thoughts from? Let me show you what John the Apostle says.

> This is the message we have heard from him and declare to you: God is light; in him there is no darkness at all. If we claim to have fellowship with him and yet walk in the darkness, we lie and do not live out the truth. But if we walk in the light, as he is in the light, we have fellowship with one another, and the blood of Jesus, his Son, purifies us from all sin.

> If we claim to be without sin, we deceive ourselves and the truth is not in us. If we confess our sins, he is faithful and just and will forgive us our sins and purify us from all unrighteousness. If we claim we have not sinned, we make him out to be a liar and his word is not in us. (1 John 1:5–10)

One problem the children of God in the Old Testament endured was that the word of God was not "in" them. It was words. It was laws. It was truth. But the people didn't take it to heart. They grumbled. They built idols. They took up foreign religions. Their hearts were quite resistant to obedience. Their spirits were led astray.

If you are feeling uneasy about what I'm talking about, that is good news. It's because you are listening. Yes, you are reading, but you are considering what God is saying to you. You are hearing from the Holy Spirit, the Spirit of Holiness, the Spirit of Truth, and he is going to impress upon you what he wants to say. After all, he will guide you, teach you, comfort you, and strengthen you. You are not living life on your own. He is with you. Maybe your work habits aren't right. Maybe your relationship skills are truly poor. Perhaps your parenting is lacking impact. Whatever your inadequacies, he intends to help you.

We realize we have been redeemed by the blood of Christ—cleansed by him. You have an assignment now in life wherever you are. You might be teaching school, you might be unemployed, you might be raising children, you might be caring for your spouse who is ill, but you're not sure of what is coming next. You don't know what the future holds. The way forward is to submit to him. Confess everything that hurts you. But trust that he has this moment. He has your eternal existence. It's like the illustration of the tango with all the dips and turns and twists. The leader doesn't lose the grip on the follower; they move together.

I can't dance for nuts. My wife can. She won a dance contest way back when we lived in Arkansas in the United States. The prize was first-class tickets for two to Auckland, New Zealand. I wasn't in the contest, obviously. I'm not even going to pretend that I can dance well. Yes! My wife took me to New Zealand. Think about this: I don't always reflect Christ the way I should, but he doesn't leave me. He helps me. He teaches me to follow his steps. So, it is with you. What are you messing up? What's got you stressed out right now?

Let's go back to Proverbs. "Trust in the Lord with all your heart and lean not on your own understanding. In all your ways submit to him, and he will make your paths straight" (Proverbs 3:5–6).

That's what we need. Sometimes we submit in small ways. Other times, submission is more personal. Baptism is a perfect example. It is one of the most beautiful acts of submission. It can't be forced upon someone. Each person must decide when he or she is ready to dip into the covering waters. You must be the one who wants to do it. You don't do it because I force you to do it. The desire to be baptized comes from you in response to what you hear from God and his word. Let God impress upon your heart. Follow on. Listen to God.

Submission is one of the most difficult areas of your life. Thankfully, not many of you dance like I do. None of you will have the same story I have. I don't have your story either. When you let the Holy Spirit lead you, he will take you places you never thought possible.

CHAPTER 4

PROVISION

There is a wonderful story of Peter walking on the water in Matthew 14:22–33. It's an interesting story because, other than Jesus, he was the only one to do so. It's only when Peter saw the mess that the storm was creating that he panicked and began to sink. Jesus had to reach out to him and rescue him from certain death. Our lives can be like this too. We charge out with good intentions only to doubt that we really can do what we need to do. The principle that I'm talking about in this chapter is provision. It is an extremely important aspect of salvation that we need to hang on to.

Providence or the provision of God is ultra-important. The reason is that you might focus on a religion and miss the awesomeness of God.

In my marriage, I have become aware of God moving in many different scenarios. Many years ago, Cami was hired to work as a receptionist in a travel agency in North Little Rock, Arkansas. While the owner of the agency was traveling across the country, she got stuck in an airport and needed to reroute her trip. This was in the days of early desktop computers. The owner called her office hoping that one of her agents would solve the problem, but the agents were out; they had all taken lunch at the same time. The boss was unimpressed. Cami offered to help her. Even though Cami didn't have a clue about what to do, the boss talked her through the process. Cami's boss was delighted that Cami displayed an aptitude for what was required, and she immediately began a training process so that Cami could become a travel agent. While some people might consider this insignificant, we recognize it as a pivotal moment in Cami's life in which God's hand was involved. This is God's provision.

God had promised Abraham land. While Abraham got to live on the land, it wasn't until Joshua took over from where Moses left off that God's promise was fulfilled. Joshua was told to enter the Promised Land. He was told that wherever he stepped foot, he would be given victory. He certainly went into battle over the land, but God's hand was with him to give him what was provided. The occupants of the land were morally polluted and, in a sense, Joshua was cleansing the land. The land consisted of gardens and vineyards. It was the land described as flowing with milk and honey. It was set up already. God gave the land to the promised people. The people had wandered around the desert, and suddenly, they experienced a bounty of goodness. It was something they had no way of providing for themselves.

Years later, David became king of Judah. Some time after that, he became the king of Israel. While that appointment alone was at the hand of God, it was the next phase of his life that astounds me. David decided to live in Jerusalem. Jerusalem was inhabited by the Jebusites, and they had no interest in allowing David to take their city. They laughed at the idea that he could even get in there, but he put forward the problem to his commanders and let them solve the problem. It turns out that the soldiers took Jerusalem by entering the city through the water system shafts. David took control of the city and named it the City of David. While I see the hand of God in this development, it was the following story that displays God providing for his anointed. The king of Tyre built a palace for David. Of all the things to happen, David knew God was with him (2 Samuel 5:6–12).

In the last chapter, I wrote about the exile of Judah. Among those exiled to Babylon was a character named Nehemiah who was made a slave and ended up working for King Artaxerxes. He became the official wine taster for the king. His role was to test the wine in case someone had spiked the king's drink with poison. Nehemiah was expendable. One day he found out that, after the Babylonian siege of Jerusalem, the city of David had been destroyed and burned. He was devastated by the news and desperately wanted to do something about it. He had a genuine love for God and the city of David. The problem was that he was far from Jerusalem and a captive. It was his desire to return to Jerusalem and fix what desperately needed to be restored. He prayed that God would enable him to do this, and he started by asking Artaxerxes to allow him to do the task.

The story is an amazing account of providence. Artaxerxes saw that Nehemiah was sad. More than likely they had developed a good relationship, and so Artaxerxes asked why Nehemiah looked upset. Nehemiah told him what was in his heart and what he needed to do. The first question from Artaxerxes concerned when Nehemiah would return from his mission. So not only did Nehemiah receive permission to fulfil his quest to restore Jerusalem, Artaxerxes successfully requisitioned supplies and references necessary to do what he needed to do. This is a seemingly impossible story. An enemy king gave a slave the means to accomplish his foreign mission. Nehemiah's story displays God's provision (Nehemiah 2:1–10).

These stories are reminders that God helps us do all sorts of things in our lives if there is something that he wants us to do. You must realize that there are some things in our lives that we can't possibly do, but God makes a way for what is impossible to take place.

When we try to understand the good news of God that is the gospels' message, it's good to be able to see that God provides salvation. When we also understand that this is, in fact, something we could never do for ourselves, we begin to appreciate the mystery of God found in provision.

Let's consider a passage from Romans: "Therefore, just as sin entered the world through one man, and death through sin, and in this way, death came to all people, because all sinned" (Romans 5:12). This text paints a clear picture: Through Adam, sin came into being. And, a result of sin, death came into being. If you were going to tell your friends about sin, where would you start? *Sin* a common term. We use it all the time. But how can we make sense out of the complexities and foibles of sin in our world? This is important because we recognize death is connected to our sin.

I want to share an analogy with you. Let's say I decided to go to the grocery store to buy "seafood." *Seafood* is the term that covers a wide range of products that come from the world's oceans. I might like to try some snapper or octopus or shrimp or shark or oysters. You get the picture. *Seafood* is a general term; it refers to a food that we can eat, but it does not refer to a specific variety of that food. In that same vein of thinking, *sin* is a general term for everything that is introduced into the Earth that is not right. When you start to grasp how big the problem of sin is, purely as an analogy, imagine how big the ocean is and just how many varieties of seafood exist. In the world, sin entered humanity; it flooded every part of our being. It's in our culture—our nations, our families, and in us personally. The world is inundated with sin.

Consider your own sin. You have some imperfections that other people don't have. You may not see exactly what's wrong with you, but others certainly recognize that you are not perfect. No one is. I think we can often see sin in someone else. We can see where they are corrupt. But we can be blind to our own "messed-up-ness." However, when we start to really examine ourselves, we begin to recognize that our problems are not simple. We have deep-seated issues that lurk beneath the surface. The whole world is like this. You are not singularly endowed with sin; we all share this predicament. This is often described as our sin problem.

We try to live out good lives, follow the Bible, and do all the right things. Take, for example, good Christian parents who have several children. Two of them are apprehended for shoplifting. The parents are super surprised; they are not delighted. "How did this happen?" The parents feel as if they have raised their kids right, and their behavior reflects poorly on them. The parents are embarrassed; the kids are ashamed (especially about being caught). The policeman talks to the children and asks typical questions. Were you hungry? Are you looking for a thrill? The kids say those are not their reasons for stealing the ice cream treats. When the policeman asks them why they did it, the kids say they don't know.

This is a typical scenario, and I think the kids are honestly telling the truth. This is like an octopus in the seafood analogy. They are not as common as fish, but there are plenty around. What about the child that tells the mother a lie? The mom says, "Why did you say that?" The child says, "I didn't say anything." The mother is instantly frustrated, and says, "Yes, you did!" The child denies not only the lie but also saying anything. It's like a vicious circle. Each child is unique. And each child's seafood basket is his or her own. The problem with mothers is that they don't fall for everything hook, line, and sinker. They can see right through their own children. I mean, did you ever try to lie to your mom? Here is a fact. More than likely she knew what you were doing. Moms have that quality. Why? How can moms know this? Well, it's because moms have their own sin problems. They grew up in sin. They know sin first hand. They went there before you. Sin is their experience. They have their own fish—lots of different ones.

Please understand that I don't struggle with the same things you struggle with. I don't have your shrimp. You don't have my shark.

Sin, as dealt with in the Bible, is a blanket term. It is used to describe all wrongdoing against God the way we use *seafood* to describe all the food from the ocean. And this is what sin is—it's action against God.

The more aware you become of your own life, the more you realize that there is something wrong with you. As you grow up, you don't want to admit it because you want to appear as someone who has it together. It's as if we wear a mask all the time. We want people to see who we are only to a certain degree. Even when we think we are being transparent, we tell people whatever we want to tell them; it doesn't mean they get the true picture. The perception is that, if children are raised in churches, they are meant to be good kids. It's as if we think children can be wrapped in Bubble Wrap and preserved from the full impact of sin. The truth is that each child is filled with sin that is waiting to get out. The problem is that even parents think they are raising good kids because their well-behaved children reflect their awesomeness. They think messed-up kids are negative reflections on them. This may not be the case. Kids will be kids. They will have some terrific days. Even though some kids are truly well nurtured, they are never without sin. We are all inundated with a sin problem. The truth is that we are messed up, and we need the awesome work of the Holy Spirit to bring Christ into our lives.

Take, for instance, those who are drawn into alcoholism. That becomes their tuna. It's a massive battle. It takes over their lives. They struggle with it. Just when they think they have it mastered, it raises its head and breaks free into the whitewash of family fall-outs. It's a deep problem. You may not struggle with that sin. It's not just a sickness. It's what the Bible calls sin. Or what about drugs? That is a huge problem in the world. You might be glad that you are not one of "those people." One day that person finds themselves in a group and says, "I'm Jane Doe, and I'm an alcoholic!" All the people applaud. Why? Because they can identify with the struggle. They have something in common. They know that it takes a great deal of courage for a person to come to a meeting and share his or her seafood with others. It's like a whole group of oysters meeting together.

The problem in church is that people forget they have fundamental issues that stick out like fins on great white sharks. There is something wrong with us. There is something wrong with me. It's not that you can see it in me. It's there. It's true. Just as sin entered the world through Adam, it has affected the whole planet. Look at nations that are messed up. Go to the Sudan and see how messed up people become— children fighting in wars with machine guns. We are ruining the planet with all kinds of pollution. This is all sin. It's the same category.

"For if by the trespass of one man, death reigned through that one man, how much more will those who receive God's abundant provision of grace and of the gift of righteousness reign in life through the one man, Jesus Christ!" (Romans 5:17). That verse sums up the good news of God. It is extraordinary news about the abundant provision of God. It's good news. If your version of the gospel isn't good news, it's not the gospel. It might just be your religious take on what you think matters to you, but it may not be the good news. There is the problem that went into every nation, every tribe, and every tongue. All that aside, there is something that came through Jesus Christ and into the world. Jesus Christ came into the world to be the sacrifice for sin. He was the one designated by God to take away the sin of the entire world. He did it. It's done. It's finished. He was the lamb of God that took away the sin of the world. He didn't just take away some of your sins. No, he took away the sin of the world. Forgiveness is in him. He took everything—all the seafood. He got it all. He came in and cleaned out the lot. He didn't miss a thing. He reached into planet Earth, and he took all sin upon himself. He took the sin on the cross. He died for the sin of the world.

We need to see how big this is. I know the analogy of seafood is a bit odd, but he took all the seafood out of the sea. None is left. Can you feel the weight of this? Of course, you can't! It was never upon your shoulders. We need to see this. For instance, we may have favorite sins—gossip, for example. You may not want to give that one up. You like it. It serves you with your friends; you take it to go. It's as if I'm going on a trip with the Holy Spirit and I've got two bags packed. I might have pride in one bag and greed in the other. I'm so used to them that I can't do without them. I can't put them down because I'm so used to unpacking them as soon as I reach my favorite place. And that might well be church on Sunday.

We need to remember God's abundant provision and righteousness. This was freely given after a great price was paid.

We need to get excited about God's all-encompassing provision of salvation and righteousness through the extraordinariness of Jesus Christ.

We recognize how all-encompassing sin is from Adam, and so we don't need to discount how all-encompassing God's grace is given through Jesus; otherwise, we struggle with a few problems like worry or gossip, and they become our favorite sins. And we don't want to give those up. We want to keep our sins. Christ's reign in our lives is all about a right relationship with God—a relationship free from rubbish.

When we try to explain the gospel story to our friends, we need to make sure that we never miss the fact that salvation has been provided. It has been given. Do you realize that I can explain the gospel story to little children, and they get it? They do! Kids aren't like adults who have become hardened by sin's deceitfulness. If little kids can understand this story, why do we think it has to be complicated? A little child can hear the gospel and understand it. So, it must be with us. We need to know our predicament. Sin is in the world, and it's got me too. I didn't miss this one. I'm inundated with sin. My problem is not just that I'm guilty, but I will have an eternal punishment because of my sin. You might say, "But I just had a few oysters!" Or, "I tasted a little catfish." You might be defensive and state, "I didn't have a shark!" The problem sin plays out in our thinking is that we compare sins as a way of downplaying our guilt: "I'm not as bad as that person." "Thank goodness, I don't have their problems." "I'm actually a pretty good person!"

The gospel story needs to hit home in each person's mind. Our thinking needs to be accurate. You need to be saying to yourself, *I'm lost in this overwhelming sea of sin. I'm drowning in my sin.* Only then will you see what God provided for all of us. You must grasp what he provided for you.

For God so loved the world that he gave his one and only son, whosever believes in him shall not perish, but have everlasting life. For God did not send his son into the world to condemn the world but he sent him to save the world through him. (John 3:16–17)

We should be jumping up and shouting about how good God is. If we have his Spirit leading us anywhere, we should be asking God for help or be yelling out our thanks from the bottom of our hearts. Jesus dying on a cross is not some sad-sack story; it means salvation for you and for me. What you have plaguing you and destroying you has been taken by Jesus Christ. You will reign with him forever. Your future is sealed with him. The almighty God himself has bestowed his great gift on you. By his grace, his goodness, and his love for you, you have been saved from the penalty of your sin. God provided this for you. You couldn't do this for yourself. You could not take away your sins. You couldn't do it. If you could have, you would have, but you can't. This is the great work of God. You might think you could have lived out a better life. No! You couldn't have. This life is drowning in sin. It was something within you. You need forgiveness by God himself. This is the way God did it. He sent a sacrifice—his own son—to pay for your sins on the cross. Jesus paid it completely. The proof is not only in scripture; it is in the fact that God is satisfied that your sin is over. It's a done deal confirmed in the resurrection of Jesus from the dead. He lives! You live! If he perished forever, you would still have your sin. It's finished. We should get excited about that fact. It's the best news ever.

When you try to understand the gospel story, you will see that it is a gift that is to be received. It's not simply information.

Remember the story of David? David received the city of David. God provided something for him that he never worked for. In that same way, you receive this new life. It is given to you when you believe in his one and only son. You take it by faith. You believe this to be true. If you deviate from this message of provision, if you add anything to it by thinking that somehow you are going to do something to make your relationship with God better, you miss out on the whole point of provision. You miss the provision. This is something impossible for you to do. You can't make yourself right with God. God made you right with him.

This message should sound out from the depths of your soul. Yes! Because it is an extraordinary message. When you are trying to figure out all the struggles you are going through in the complexity of your life, you must come back to the fact that someone has gone before you to provide a way out of whatever is sinking you. Jesus says, come, if you are thirsty (Revelation 22:17). And you come simply by believing in Jesus. Jesus, I need that life that you give. It is freely given. It is a gift of life. This is what is important about the gospel.

In the concept of convergence, you can't leave this principle of providence out. It's the bedrock of your steps. If you ignore it, you will just end up with a religious story. You will end up focusing on your religion. You will forget about the extraordinariness of Jesus Christ, and you will be all about some manmade agenda. We are all the same. Yes, we have had different experiences. You might have struggled with something that I didn't have to worry about. You may not be able to tell me everything about yourself or your true struggles. I'll struggle with things I will never tell you about either. Some things in me you may not like. You might not like that I am grumpy when I'm tired. The good part of this story is not about how good I am. The good part of the story is how good God is! God loves you while you are a sinner. He loves you. He knew you before the beginning of time. There are some extraordinary things about the mystery of Christ.

In this Spirit-led journey of life, don't forget provision.

CHAPTER 5

WAITING

The Holy Spirit is a person, not simply a power and a force. For us to understand God's work in our lives, we can't forget the personal aspects. The theme of this chapter is not only personal, it could be a very tender area for you to consider.

The principle of convergence we will consider in this chapter is the idea of waiting. I'm not a fan of waiting, but it's not only a normal part of life, it is also infused in our spiritual journey. We learn that, in all things, God works for good, and sometimes we question what this means, but it's important to hold the thought of something good being drawn out through waiting.

Our local church runs a small café, and my awareness of good coffee has grown over the years. If you think about instant coffee, you will see that it's easy, quick, and relatively inexpensive. The taste is predictable, but if you make an instant coffee you have very little influence over how good that coffee can be. However, making an espresso coffee will change your coffee experience.

I grew up in a valley in Papua New Guinea where coffee farming became popular, and my father was involved in pioneering coffee processing. In fact, one of my first jobs was buying local coffee from the farmers for a processing factory. I never thought it would play a role in my ministry, but it has. Every coffee-growing region in the world has different conditions that influence the flavor and aroma of coffee. I can always identify coffee that comes from Papua New Guinea because it has a distinct taste. It's not like instant coffee; it is a unique coffee.

In some ways, my experience has formulated my taste awareness, but working as a barista in the church café over the past several years has made me think about why some coffee tastes better than others. A good espresso machine extracts the best flavor possible from each type of coffee (not instant coffee). The temperature of the water must be right. The flavor is extracted under pressure. The beans must be ground to the right consistency. The time of the extract is approximately twenty-five seconds. Interestingly enough, different flavors and qualities come through at different times. The first part of the pour may extract a fruity taste. This is followed by an acidic balance in the middle and finished off by the right amount of bitterness that is necessary for good coffee. This perfect convergence results in a good coffee.

Why am I telling you all this? Well, we can compare coffee to the spiritual influences in our lives. We may think we like instant spirituality, but God chooses to pour his Spirit through what comes together in our lives. He is not in a hurry. We may be; he is not. We often must wait for his approach in drawing out our best.

The more you drink good coffee, the more aware you will be of what good coffee really is. People who drink instant coffee may like the taste of their brand of coffee, but they don't really get the nuanced perfection that good coffee can create. It's not just about drinking a coffee, it's about savoring the goodness brought forth through a creative process.

When it comes to the intimacy of God in our lives, I'm interested in the richness that he brings. We are talking about God residing in the well-being of our entire lives. I think for many years of my life I've been a bit of an "instant Christian" sort of guy. Going to church was a necessary part of life. I did it, but I wasn't too interested in knowing how things came about. The church is God's converging community, and it brings about the best out of our lives.

When you look at the oldest parts of scriptures, you come across many characters who knew what it was like to wait. Moses was one of those people. He ran away from Egypt and lived in the desert. He had been a big shot in Egypt with a great education, but he found himself living in fear for his life in the wilderness. He reinvented himself as a shepherd and spent forty years as a nomadic herdsman. He lost his prominence. In that "back-burner experience," God prepared him for the next phase of his life. In the next phase, he was leading the nation of Israel out of Egypt and into a forty-year trek in the desert. He was humbled by God. He never got to lead the people into the Promised Land. Much of his journey with God was shaped through waiting. He wasn't the only one.

Elijah was a prophet who led an amazing life. He challenged the prophets of Baal. In the challenge, he asked God to rain down fire to burn up his sacrifice. God did so. It was awesome and amazing—a real highlight in his life. In the process of taking on the establishment of the day, Elijah made Queen Jezebel mad. She threatened to kill him. He ran away and fell into a state of overwhelming depression. He felt as if he was all alone against evil in the world. Essentially, he was done with life. He was waiting to die. In his waiting, God ministered to him, physically, mentally, and spiritually. Elijah understood waiting. God made good out of evil.

The story of David is a grand reminder that even the favorite servants of God spend a whole lot of time waiting. As a boy, David was anointed by Samuel the prophet but didn't know what the anointed task would be. It may have been fifteen years before David became king of Judah and then later king of Israel. There was a time in a cave when King Saul was trying to kill him that David practiced waiting. He was in the cave hiding, and Saul was standing beside him totally unaware of how vulnerable his life was, but David chose to wait and not kill Saul. David did what was right. He waited until God moved him into his role as king.

I think my favorite waiting person may be Paul the Apostle. He was introduced as Saul in the book of Acts. In the beginning, he was waiting in the wings of a hostile crowd listening to the sermon of Stephen. He was seething with anger as a self-appointed servant of righteousness. He hated the Christian development and made it his personal mission to destroy Christians. He thought he was doing God a favor by cleansing the earth of the upstart movement coming out of the Jews.

We learn about the change in Saul when he met Jesus in some sort of spiritual enlightenment on his way from Jerusalem up to the city of Damascus. He was a man thinking he was doing what God wanted him to do, but God met him on that road and forever changed him for good. He was renamed Paul. Through a radical series of converging events, Paul was commissioned to be an ambassador for Jesus Christ to the gentile people in the various nations. He didn't get to go right away. We learn that he went into the desert and spent three years receiving personal instruction from Jesus. This is a challenging concept because Jesus was in heaven but was also instructing Paul. I imagine this was a solitary time with God that was directly influenced by the Spirit of Christ.

While people say different things about the time line of Paul's life, I've calculated that there may have been as much as fourteen years between his commission by Christ and the time that he embarked on what is called his first mission trip. That was a long period of waiting for someone I don't picture to be overly patient.

Paul was a leader in the early Christian movement, but he also spent a whole lot of time in prison. He was often in prison or under house arrest. Paul was a prime advocate for furthering the case of Christ. He was a preacher with a confronting message. Paul was outspoken. It got him in trouble quite often when the different authorities took offense to Paul's message and incarcerated him. He spent a great deal of time waiting in prison.

While Paul was in prison, he wrote letters. This is where we get so much of the New Testament from. If I'm feeling down, I'm not likely to look to the book of Jeremiah for inspiration. The prophet Jeremiah seemed to be often depressed, and so he focused on all that was wrong. If you look at the impact he had, you'll see that not too many people listened to his instruction. He was in some ways negative, and so his work can be a bit distressing if you read it when you are not up to comprehending what he was writing about. No, the first book I go to be uplifted is Paul's letter to the Philippian church. Paul was in prison writing the letter and reminding people to rejoice always—an amazing perspective from a man who learned that, while he waited, God would extract good.

Paul had a deep work of the Holy Spirit in his life. He understood whom he served and what was ultimately important. He understood his existence, why he was on planet Earth, and what his life was all about.

In the book of Ephesians, Paul surprises me with a few well-placed words:

> Pray also for me, that whenever I speak, words may be given me so that I will fearlessly make known the mystery of the gospel, for which I am an ambassador in chains. Pray that I may declare it fearlessly, as I should. (Ephesians 6:19–20)

I'm surprised because that isn't the way I see Paul. I don't ever see him as one who feared what people thought about what he said. I see him as a hero of the faith, charging into every opportunity to share the gospel. Not so. Paul knew that he didn't always get it right. The message was right. His gospel was spot on. The problem he faced was plain old fear of rejection. He asked the church to pray for him so that he could be as "flavorful" as possible.

Sometimes, Christianity can seem like instant coffee. We go through the motions of something that doesn't force us to examine not only why this life is so good, but also how it is extracted to bring about the greater good. This life is a spiritual journey. We are going somewhere. We are led by the Holy Spirit. It is important that we are in sync with developments. So, God is extracting his good from you in the times of waiting. I almost hate that word—*waiting*.

When Cami and I had been married just a little over two years, we moved from Corpus Christi, Texas, to Jacksonville, Arkansas. It was all new for us. It was a very difficult place for a foreigner to find acceptance and certainly to put down roots. We tried several churches, but I didn't care much for church. You might say I was uninterested in church. My wife was concerned for me and certainly for us. She joined ladies' groups wherever we went, and she confided in some of these new friends her concerns for me. She began to pray for me. Her prayer was that I would become the spiritual leader of the household. She prayed the prayer for about fifteen years.

Even though I wasn't interested in church, I got the urge to join the First Baptist Church in Jacksonville, Arkansas. The main reason I wanted to go to that church was to further my business. I had already joined the local Chamber of Commerce and had learned that quite a few prominent business leaders attended that church.

It didn't take too long for someone to ask if we would teach in the retirement home for the elderly. The lady who approached us seemed to feel that we could be useful in that ministry, but, I think they asked everybody who came along to get involved. Immediately, I knew my cover was blown. I knew very little about Christianity at the time; however, I did believe in the saving work of Jesus. While I had been raised in a thoroughly Christian home, I had always been a fringe attendant in activities. Cami thought we should get involved, so we began a ministry every second Sunday morning teaching in an old folks' home. I'm not sure what I taught. I don't think too many heard much, but it was a launching place for my Bible beginnings.

Our work with the elderly was extremely taxing. We would grow attached to lovely old dears only to come along on different occasions to learn that there was a new soul in the recently departed bed. It was hard work. I take responsibilities seriously, and I worked at the home for several years.

There was a young couple working with teenagers in the church, and a fellow named Patrick asked me to teach students in year ten. Again, I knew I was totally inadequate for the role, but he was extremely persuasive, so I switched from eighty-five-year-olds to teenagers. I don't know that they heard much more, but I found I was greatly interested in the work.

All the while (unbeknownst to me), Cami was still praying for me to become the spiritual leader of our household. She was faithfully waiting for much more to come out of me.

It turns out that the people in this church knew how to recruit people for different assignments, and my efforts were being added daily to whatever was going on. Before long I became a church bus driver, and eventually I became a deacon. Cami kept praying and waiting for the family to have a spiritual leader.

The problem with teaching so many classes and attending every church service going was that God does his work through every means possible. This church held revival meetings during which a guest preacher would stir up people like me. Even the pastor knew how to get inside my head with all sorts of questions and thoughts.

While there had been a few developments that caused our relocation to Australia, God was preparing me for what Cami was waiting for. The move made me question who I was and why I was feeling personally challenged. I had all sorts of issues that resulted in various emotional responses, including anger, that I had wrestled with for a long time.

In Australia, there was a revival meeting at a campground at Currimundi, and our church was involved. While I had been heavily involved in youth work at our new local church, I felt angry about some things that had happened, and I was feeling extremely negative when I attended the camp. The speaker was wearing a terribly ugly shirt. I felt as if he was preaching a different gospel than the one I knew. Inside I was cranky. All sorts of feelings went through me. The power in the room was so strong that I couldn't stay inside. It was a holiness factor. I was an unholy mess, and God was very present in a holy way.

I went outside by myself and began to cry. My state of mind was strangely shattered; I was emotionally distraught. I don't mean to make this experience seem weird. I was just going through a very difficult but extremely powerful moment.

The next afternoon, a friend contacted me and invited me to a men's prayer group. These men helped me to process some of what I'd been going through. As they prayed for me, suddenly, I felt as if all my troubles had evaporated. I left the prayer time with a peace way beyond anything I had ever experienced. The truth was that the revival had totally transformed me.

Remember that my wife had been praying that I would become the spiritual leader in the family. Sometimes I wish she hadn't prayed that prayer, but she did. It was her "fault" that things converged together for good. God listened to her and moved in on me.

How many years did she wait? I don't think she knows. Finally, there came a time when she asked herself why she was praying the prayer.

Ultimately, I decided to go to Bible college. The interviewing principal asked me why I thought I should be at bible college. I told him I didn't know. Understand that I never intended to be considered for pastoral ministry. I felt that it was an imperative in my life—something that I just had to do. The principal told me that they would soon know why I was there. I nearly left college the first week because it was so hard. After I had completed several semesters, the lecturer of theology came to me and told me that I was a preacher. I'm not sure why he said that. He gave me several preaching assignments in the southeast corner of Queensland. In my final year, I preached thirty-two times in six different denominations. My son, Syd, travelled with me. We saw some extraordinary movements of God.

My daughter, Katrina, was going through some identity issues in her early teenage life. She was born smart. But life has a way of showing us that there are always other people who are smarter. She wrestled internally. One morning she walked to the front of the church in tears. She was a broken young lady who needed healing. Cami and I went with her. We have always been a close family. Her testimony years later was that, in that season of her life, she witnessed powerful changes in my life, and she knew that trusting God with her life would bring her to a right spiritual place. She was right.

Some years after that, my son, Syd was going through his own personal dramas in life. While he had decided to accept Christ when he was a young boy, he found himself disappointed at college and withdrew into himself. He came to me one afternoon and told me that he needed help. He knew that sin had become a problem in his life. I prayed with him. That afternoon of prayer resulted in a man transformed by God himself. Within a few months, he came to me again and told me that he wanted to devote his life to doing what I do. "Dad, you help people." He is involved in fulltime vocational ministry.

Waiting. Waiting. How many times do you think nothing is happening in your life, but really, in the background, there are things coming together? God is often drawing things out of your life making way for what comes next.

There is a passage in Revelation about waiting. It's a revelation to a church. It speaks to people in that church individually and collectively. The message is that Jesus wants to restore what isn't right. The person waiting is Jesus. The agent of change is the Holy Spirit through holy action.

> To the angel of the church in Laodicea write:
> These are the words of the Amen, the faithful
> and true witness, the ruler of God's creation. I
> know your deeds, that you are neither cold nor
> hot. I wish you were either one or the other!
> So, because you are lukewarm—neither hot nor
> cold—I am about to spit you out of my mouth.
> (Revelation 3:14–16)

It's a simple everyday illustration. It's referring to people in the church. They are busy. However, the people themselves are distasteful to Jesus. Cold water is refreshing on a hot day. Hot water is therapeutic or healing. An iced coffee is refreshing. A hot coffee is comforting. A lukewarm coffee has zero appeal. It should be one or the other: hot or cold. Christian activity is good, but it should either be refreshing or healing, never neither. The problem is what exists within everyone.

> You say, "I am rich; I have acquired wealth and
> do not need a thing." But you do not realize that
> you are wretched, pitiful, poor, blind and naked.
> I counsel you to buy from me gold refined in
> the fire, so that you can become rich; and white
> clothes to wear, so that you can cover your
> shameful nakedness; and salve to put on your
> eyes, so that you can see. (Revelation 3:17–18)

People in Laodicea were self-sufficient. They were spiritually depleted. The problem was that they had no clue about their true spiritual condition. None. So, Jesus asks them to invest in his reviving work. They were empty and had lost the hunger and thirst for Jesus himself. For him, this was true wealth, not self-determinism. In the refining processes of gold, impurities come to the surface through heat. His fire is hot. The result is his clothing of forgiveness rather than self-validated spirituality. Whatever was shameful would be addressed. Only then can people see what he wants them to see. The offer is for us too: revival. Nothing less.

> Those whom I love I rebuke and discipline. So be earnest and repent. Here I am! I stand at the door and knock. If anyone hears my voice and opens the door, I will come in and eat with that person, and they with me. (Revelation 3:19–20)

Most people think this is a verse to non-Christians. It's a rebuke to whoever will listen. Jesus is patient. He is waiting outside the heart. We must offer a heartfelt and sincere response to Jesus himself. Without a change of mind, nothing good will result. It's really a verse to the church. The result will be an intimate fellowship individually and corporately.

> To the one who is victorious, I will give the right to sit with me on my throne, just as I was victorious and sat down with my Father on his throne. Whoever has ears, let them hear what the Spirit says to the churches. (Revelation 3:21–22)

Not everyone is going to get this, but if we listen and genuinely respond to what he is saying, there will be good outcomes.

Some can find themselves self-satisfied in life: Good career. Comfortable living conditions. No experience of lack. The problem is that some people do not realize what is happening in their lives. In the spirituality picture these people are like lukewarm instant coffee. God doesn't want it. He would spit out what these people represent.

There is stuff about all of us that is messed up, and we don't even know it. We can't know it. We might argue that we would know where we stand with God, but in this passage, we see that there is a good chance we could be delusional about out right standing with God. We go through the motions. Church can become like instant coffee. We drink it because that's what we quickly do, but we don't listen to what he is truly saying. How is God working on the inside of our lives? How is he drawing out the good, even in the waiting? Sometimes we are held over the fire for a reason. God is not in a hurry.

You might be in a place that you never thought you would be. Maybe it's a job that is miserable. Here is the truth: God will bring something good out of you. You are more important to God than anything you will ever do. So often we want our big assignment in life, and we tell God that we are ready for our mission. Moses found there was a lot of waiting in life. And circumstances didn't always work out the way he thought they were going to work out.

Paul the Apostle wanted to go to Spain and to Rome. We don't know how far he got. He wanted to preach in Rome. I don't think prison was his first choice. Some people think he may have ventured as far as Wales. What we do know is that Paul spent a whole lot of time waiting—waiting to do some of the things he wanted to do.

Are you waiting for God to do something for you or in your life? You might be asking why it's taking so long. Maybe you are waiting for promises to come to fruition. Sometimes people are waiting for children to come to faith. I wonder if sometimes you don't miss the point that Christ is waiting for you. He is waiting for you to answer the knock on your heart. He wants to be in his rightful place in your life.

I'm not sure how many times in your life that you will need a touch by God, but I would say there will be many times he will seek to speak to you. You might not be as together in Christ as you think you are; yet, you will hear his voice. When was the last time you experienced revival in your life? Are you overdue for revival? Is the waiting pointing to what needs refreshing or healing? So many times, we dwell on what we think is important in life, but it is Christ himself who is of supreme importance. If Paul was willing to ask a church to pray for him in his waiting, we need to be willing to admit we need people to pray for us. You were never meant to live life alone. You were made with an internal intimate capacity to be with God. His holy extraction of you will bring out his best in you. It takes time.

Chapter 6

Tasks

One easy Saturday morning I was in my shed working out what art project was next. I heard a screech coming from one of the ladies of the house. It turns out that Cami, my ever-observant wife, discovered that a carpet snake was resting beside the pool right beneath her lounge chair. She wasn't interested in sharing the space or the moment with Jake. (It doesn't matter what name a snake goes by, Cami always refers to them as Jake.) She wanted him or her gone, and I was assigned the task of moving this character on. I could have called a snake catcher to come and do what they do, but no, I knew it was my job.

I went looking for my trusty welding gloves (that have never seen a welding project), but alas, they were nowhere to be found. So, I decided that a nice garden waste sack would have to be my weapon of choice. I approached the snake, who had decided to move behind the air conditioner unit, and planned my attack. The unsuspecting snake met its match. Its head was hanging out one side of the unit and its tail was hanging out the other. I placed an open sack in front of its furiously wagging tongue and went around and tickled its tail. With four moves, the six-foot-long snake was all the way coiled up inside the sack. I grabbed the sack and gathered the opening together. I then placed the sack in a wheelie trash bin and promptly drove fifteen minutes away to the other side of the river and released it. Now this sounds all brave and courageous, but the truth was that I had some reservations. What drove me to success was the desire to win despite my feelings and fears. I was a bit scared along the way.

God designed people in such a way that work is part of life. Work will always be meaningful, and we learn very early on that work plays a huge part in our lives. Even in paradise, Adam was expected to work. From that work he would experience more of God's expectations for his life. We, too, have been created to work, and God will give us assignments. Our lives are made up of specific tasks at different times. Catching a snake may be a very ordinary task, but I'm writing about more than the everyday projects. I want to address your God-given tasks in this Spirit-led journey.

If I were to tell you the story of Joshua and his God-given task of leading the Israelites into the Promised Land, you might recall the scriptures that reminded Joshua to be brave and courageous. What we often overlook is what took place before he received that assignment. If you read the last bit of Deuteronomy, you will notice a whole lot about what Joshua went through in preparation for his God-given task. Moses prepared the people for God's expectations of what was in store for them once they departed from their season in the desert.

> Then Moses climbed Mount Nebo from the plains of Moab to the top of Pisgah, opposite Jericho. There the Lord showed him the whole land—from Gilead to Dan, all of Naphtali, the territory of Ephraim and Manasseh, all the land

of Judah as far as the Mediterranean Sea, the Negev and the whole region from the Valley of Jericho, the City of Palms, as far as Zoar. Then the Lord said to him, "This is the land I promised on oath to Abraham, Isaac and Jacob when I said, 'I will give it to your descendants.' I have let you see it with your eyes, but you will not cross over into it." (Deuteronomy 34:1-4)

This is a story of the transition of leadership from Moses to Joshua. Moses had led the most extraordinary life possible. He had accomplished all sorts of amazing things. For forty years he had lived as a shepherd like a nomad of the desert. He had plenty of time to think about his life and the situation of his people back in Egypt. Then God gave him the assignment for his life. He was told to go and rescue the people from Egypt. He went to Egypt and served God through displays of God's awesome power. Remember the terrible plagues, the decisive Passover exodus, and then the crossing of the Red sea. Once in the desert, the people had a choice to go on to the Promised Land, but they decided it was all too hard and so they never went in. For forty years Moses led the Israelites around in the desert until this new moment in time. The problem for Moses was that God showed him the land from a distance, but God was not going to allow Moses the chance to go in.

And Moses the servant of the Lord died there in Moab, as the Lord had said. He buried him in Moab, in the valley opposite Beth Peor, but to this day no one knows where his grave is. Moses was a hundred and twenty years old when he died, yet his eyes were not weak nor his strength gone. The Israelites grieved for

Moses in the plains of Moab thirty days, until
the time of weeping and mourning was over.
(Deuteronomy 34:5–8)

Who buried him? We learn that God himself buried him.
The people didn't bury Moses. Moses went up to see a panorama
of what was ahead, and then he died. Remember, God is Spirit,
and God buried him. This is good for us to grasp. When we are
trying to understand life and the practicalities of life, we plan
things and rationalize all sorts of outcomes, but there must be
workings of God that are beyond the explainable. I'm talking
about the spiritual workings of God. When God decides to
act and to move, he chooses his way of being conventional. The
people didn't get a chance to bury Moses. It wasn't offered to
them. Moses was 120 years old, but there was nothing wrong
with Moses. He could see perfectly. He was fit. Understand, he
was 120 years old. Rationalize that! God had supernaturally
taken care of Moses. Moses had led the people for forty years.
According to their customs, the people mourned the death of
Moses. They were in shock. They were devastated. He had been
a massive figure in the community: "Now Joshua son of Nun
was filled with the spirit of wisdom because Moses had laid his
hands on him. So, the Israelites listened to him and did what
the Lord had commanded Moses" (Deuteronomy 34:9).

Think about Joshua. He had been with Moses for forty
years. The only leader he had ever known was Moses. Moses
died. Joshua was commissioned to take over. Everything had
always revolved around Moses. Joshua had always been a distant
second. Understand that Moses was awesome. Suddenly, Joshua
finds that he is to be the leader without Moses. He was still
grieving the death of Moses. He had lost Moses! Now he had
to fill sandals that were ginormous. He felt that this task was

way beyond him. I'm sure he wanted to shout that he couldn't do whatever God was calling him to do. The pressure was huge. He was going to have to be like Moses! Well, no! Not so.

> Since then, no prophet has risen in Israel like Moses, whom the Lord knew face to face, who did all those signs and wonders the Lord sent him to do in Egypt – to Pharaoh and to all his officials and to his whole land. For no one has ever shown the mighty power or performed the awesome deeds that Moses did in the sight of all Israel. (Deuteronomy 34:10–12)

Joshua didn't ever have to compare himself with Moses. Realize that the people would always compare him with Moses. A friend of Joshua might remind him, "When we ran out of water in the desert, Moses struck the rock and a river started!" Someone might remind them of Marah: "Remember when we got to the lake Marah and the water was polluted?" Another would say, "I sure do. Moses threw a stick into the water, and we ended up with pristine drinking water!" Everyone would chip in, "Moses was the best leader ever!"

Joshua had a massive calling on his life, and he had to figure out how he was going to work through it. It is the same way in your life. God has different tasks for you to do. If we tried to compare ourselves with Moses or Joshua or Paul the Apostle, we would find ourselves failing miserably. I can't compare my life with yours. And, you can't compare your life with mine. We can't compare our lives with anyone else's. God has different tasks for you to do: "For we are God's workmanship, created in Christ Jesus to do good works, which God prepared in advance for us to do" (Ephesians 2:10).

There is no doubt that God has work ahead for you. God has prepared tasks and assignments that will bring significance into your life. There will be different seasons in which these tasks will play major roles in who you are. You might feel that you are walking around in the desert. You might be. Even when the Israelites were walking around in the desert, God was taking care of them. He fed them quail and manna. Their clothes didn't wear out in forty years. Explain those ideas. We are at a loss for words. God performed the extraordinary during the very ordinary. God provided for them even when they got so much wrong. They mumbled and grumbled and built the golden calf and had snakes biting them because they sinned, yet God moved in power to preserve his overall promise of land. He took care of them. It may seem in your life that nothing is going forward, but that is not the case. There is a time for everything, and in this case, there was a time to finally enter the Promised Land.

The people had wandered around in the desert for forty years. What did they know about living in cities? What did they know about farming or tending grapevines? They had been slaves, and then they became nomads. They were displaced people. They were homeless tribes. They were about to go into a region where there were orchards and farms and vineyards. Everything was changing for them. God stopped feeding them manna. They had to grow their vegetables.

Some things must end in our lives before we experience the blessings that he will provide.

When God decided to take Moses home, he didn't take a poll to find out what the people thought. Moses died. I think we fear the agony of dying or losing a job or losing what is precious to us, but even in that, we learn that God takes care of us in his way. It was God being very personal to Moses. We have no idea how long our lives will be. We could die suddenly. There was an intimacy in how God took care of Moses, and there will be that same intimacy in how God will respond to you. He will personally care for you. However, he works the process of life, you will be in his ultimate care. Fear will encourage you to avoid the unknown, the changes and challenges that lie ahead, the conflict that is coming, and the work that you are supposed to be doing.

Fear can be a driving force in our lives. The people were worried about going into the Promised Land. It was forty years before Joshua had a look at where they had to go. He was part of a scouting group of twelve men. Ten of them knew that the task was too challenging for them. Caleb and Joshua knew that, if God wanted them to take the Promised Land, he would give them victory. For forty years he knew they missed their opportunity because their fear was powerful. Joshua knew what was ahead in that land. He had been there. The rest of them were clueless. The fear of the unknown would have been extremely powerful. Understand that they were charging into conflict. They were going to displace all the nations that called the Promised Land their own. No one was going to welcome the sea of Israelites coming into the land. They were never going to walk up to Jericho and have someone walk out with the keys to the city and say, "Come take my city! We have been waiting for you guys to show up. Come live with me."

God didn't give them a blueprint that would show them how they were going to take up residency in the Promised Land. Imagine if the church assigned a committee to pass a vote of confidence in walking around Jericho until the walls fell. No one would vote in favor of what God initiated. No one. God didn't tell them everything.

So, it is with the blueprint of your life. God doesn't tell you everything that is going to happen and how it will happen. If you had that knowledge, you would struggle to go forward. He might give you a task, but he isn't going to reveal to you every detail the way you would like him to. He is not waiting for you to read through a contract and sign off on the plans he has for you.

The problem we have is that fear can rob us of what we can do. We think, *No! The task ahead is too great.* Fear will give you great avoidance power.

Do you realize that what got you to where you are today will not get you where you are going next? There must be deaths along the way. Moses got the people to the doors of the Promised Land, but no further. Death is an ending. Dying can be painful. You will grieve when anything precious is taken away from you. Grieving is normal. No one escapes this emotional necessity. When you suffer a great loss, you must go through a genuine period of grieving marked by mourning. It could be the death of a job. You might work in a career for forty years and then retire. This is a death in your significance. Your identity is alive in what you do more than you are aware. If your work is taken away, you will feel it.

"Blessed are those who mourn, for they will be comforted" (Matthew 5:4). Do you recognize that mourning is a vehicle that will deliver comfort? A blessing is revealed at the end of a "normal" season of mourning. Mourning is not a sign of weakness. It is a requirement of life. You can't just run into the Promised Land without paying the tax of mourning.

God doesn't want you to memorialize the past. The people could have buried Moses. God could have let them pick up his body, carry it off to some unique location, and create a monument. Everyone would know where he was, and they would be forever going to visit his tomb. You can just imagine that, every time the people got upset with Joshua, they would be running off to go "talk" with Moses at his grave. They might require such a pilgrimage as part of their religion if they had half a chance. God didn't want that to happen. God didn't want them to run back to memorialize the leader who had taken them on the epic journey. God ushered in a new era.

There is one scripture that has kept me from running back away from God's work into a past life: "Jesus replied, 'No one who puts his hand to the plow and looks back is fit for service in the kingdom of God'" (Luke 9:62).

This verse has kept me going forward in ministry. There have been many times when I thought I would do everyone a favor by quitting what I was doing. Picture this: You grasp the handles of a plow in your hands. The bull attached to the plow is pulling you forward. But then you turn and look behind you. As you turn, you lose your grip on the handles, and you stumble into a rut that you were not trying to dig. You trip and fall. However, if you keep looking forward, the bull does the work, and your field is properly plowed. So, it is with our Spirit-led journey. Our eyes must be focused on where we intend to go.

The people of Israel loved looking back. There were times when they got tired of eating manna. They looked all the way back to their past and reminded themselves that, back in Egypt, they had fish, onions, leeks, and cucumbers to eat. Life was so good when they had onions to eat. Forget the fact that they were being beaten to death as slaves by the Egyptians. They had onions. It is so easy to look back and think times were so much better then.

The Holy Spirit will empower you for the tasks that lie ahead. Moses knew that Joshua needed God's power for what was ahead. When he laid his hands on him, it was a transference from one leader to a new one. God was supplying exactly what he needed: "Blessed are those who hunger and thirst for righteousness for they shall be filled" (Matthew 5:6).

There is no limit for the Spirit. Joshua would play a huge role. Moses knew it. God enabled Joshua to do what God wanted him to do. You have no limit for his power in your life. Moses loved God. It was said that he had an intimate, face-to-face relationship with God. He pressed into whatever that was. In our lives, if we hunger and thirst to walk with him, there is no limit to what he will do.

When we lived in Jacksonville, Arkansas, we were part of a group made up mostly of Australians living in Arkansas. At that time there must have been about twenty people who were from Australia, and all in all, about thirty-five people in the group. The University of Arkansas in Little Rock had a tennis program, and quite a few of their team consisted of rotating Australians. Obviously, team members were recruited through association. Different Aussies would show up from time to time.

I became friends with the players and ended up making a great friend. He was called Jimmy. Jimmy was six foot four and probably the most likeable character you could ever meet. Everyone knew him. He was a good tennis player and a standout on the team. He met and married a young lady from the university and stepped out into the real world as a happily married man. His desire was to travel on the tennis satellite tour and become a professional tennis player. I'm not sure how long that idea lasted, but it didn't work out the way he hoped. He soon found himself unable to afford to stay out on the tour. Essentially, he must have felt that he had failed as a professional, but, he didn't have the financial pool to find out just how good he really was. That development took a toll on his marriage, and I'm sure created an unfavorable situation.

Somehow, he came to work for my company as a designer because his university degree was in the graphic arts. He was very talented and the sort of person you loved to be around. His marriage ended rather suddenly. I'm not sure of the details, but his wife got involved with another fellow and unceremoniously announced that she was through. She left quickly, and Jimmy has never seen her since that day. He was smashed—totally devastated. The shock was awful. It was like a death in his life.

I spent countless hours talking with Jimmy and journeying through what had taken place. He went through a grieving process and then had to face his new reality being by himself. After some time, a new Aussie tennis player showed up at the university. Wendy was a slender, tall girl from Parkes in New South Wales, and could she play a great game. Immediately, my mate was smitten. They became friends and were unsure of what would eventually unfold. When Wendy's stint at the university concluded, she returned to Australia. Jimmy came to me and told me that he wanted to pursue his friendship with Wendy and that he would have to leave his employment to keep the girl in his sights. It was a great turn of events and certainly necessary if they had a future.

A few months after he arrived in Australia, he called me to let me know that they were engaged. The wedding was planned for February in Parkes. He asked me if I would consider being his best man. I didn't have much to think about; I was glad to stand with him at that important moment, and I treasured the fact that he wanted me to be his best man.

My own life story was also changing. For almost a year I'd had the idea that God wanted me to return to Australia. With that idea in mind, I advertised in a trade journal that my company was for sale. My wonderful office manager, Jeannean (whom Jimmy had been instrumental in hiring), found the advertisement and asked me what I was trying to do. She expressed an interest in buying the business. Three days before I flew to Australia, she handed me a check and bought the company. While this sounded great, it was extremely pressure packed. For fourteen years I had been self-employed in a business that I had pioneered. In that part of the world, I was well known, well liked, and respected. Instantly, I experienced a death in identity. I was unemployed. We often forget the fact that our work gives us a sense of satisfaction and worth. The minute work is gone, it's as if the foundation of our worth crumbles underneath us and we sink onto a floor lined with worthlessness. It may sound silly, but it's true.

I went to the wedding with all sorts of emotions holding me up. When I arrived in Parkes, I was reminded that I was supposed to make a speech. Now, I was the least likely person on the planet to give a speech. I just didn't do up-front talking—ever. While I was a bit nervous, I knew I could write out my speech and read it aloud. I would survive. On the morning of the wedding, I woke up as sick as a dog. I was messed up completely. Friends took me into town to see a physician, and he prescribed a course of whatever medication was supposed to make me well. Through the day, I did improve. I didn't write the speech because I was hopelessly wallowing in bed. It was a huge wedding. Wendy must have known everyone in Parkes, and they all showed up for the grand occasion. I managed to do my part and got through the ceremony. I was extremely weak and feeling every bit of what one feels when bit by the travel bug.

The night arrived, and the reception was about to begin. It was held in a giant white tent. The place was packed to the curtains. When it was time for my speech, I found myself on my feet with a microphone in my hand. I spoke for several minutes. The audience was mesmerized. You could have heard a pin drop on the much-trodden on grass. I concluded to a thunderous applause that literally blew me away. I knew in that moment that I was party to something far bigger than myself.

Once the speeches concluded and the formalities subsided, a young man came up to me with a sheepish grin on his face. He said, "Who are you? What do you do? Are you a politician or something?" I laughed. He then said, "I have a confession to make." I was curious. He continued, "Do you remember yesterday? I was the one who shot you."

The day before, all the men in the wedding party had all participated in the buck's party paintball adventure. We had run around like fourteen-year-old boys playing several games with various objectives, but one of the games was capturing the Australian flag. Somehow, I found myself in a position to storm the site of the flag and grab hold of it with an announcement that I had won the game. I was sprawled out on the ground waving the flag in the air when an enemy player charged up to me and stood over me spraying me with paint. It hurt like crazy. Understand that the next day I was supposed to be the best man at the front of the church, and it would be nice to be undecorated with black-and-blue bruises.

"Oh, yes! I do remember," I said. He was extremely apologetic and explained that my speech had put him under conviction for being a ratbag. He had listened to me tell the story of how Jimmy had found the love of his life and had set out to chase her until he caught her. It was an epic love story even without the inclusion of Jimmy's previous disappointment. This fellow was unhappy with himself because he had wanted to win the game and couldn't stand the fact that someone else had done so.

But after hearing my speech, he was glad that I won because he felt that I was the best kind of mate that someone could have. It was his final words that floored me. He told me what his life's work was. Sheepishly he said, "I'm a policeman!" I laughed for a good while.

I had no idea of what would unfold in my life. None. My season in Jacksonville ended. I had never thought of preaching. Well, a fleeting thought had visited me. But I had quickly dismissed it. After all, I don't do public speaking, and let's face it, preaching involves a lot of talking to a lot of people. What I learned in that moment was that there was something that God wanted me to do. God was with me. He provided everything that I needed. It was an affirmation that there was a death behind me, and I was stepping into a whole new moment in time. Right then, he showed me that he was with me.

It's the same in your life. There will be times when something comes to an end. There is closure. You may even think you are doing everything all on your own. But for what you have in front of you, you are not on your own. That is a beautiful realization. You know there is something you have to do with your life. It does come together—Your calling, your sacrifice, submission. There is a convergence. You can't compare your life with mine. Your story is not my story. Mine is not yours. There are so many things that play out in our lives. You may try to explain events mechanically or rationally. We love to make good sense. We try to figure everything out. There is a spiritual side to your reality. You cannot go through life without God himself in you. He is present to guide your very steps. There are things in your life that will change, and change will bring other things together.

The convergence of all these events and tasks can show us that there are some mysteries beyond our comprehension.

The ordinances of Christ in baptism and in communion are not memorial feasts to take us backwards in time. They lead us forward. You may be thinking you have lost something in life, and you are sinking. Baptism is a picture of your death, but not just death; it's about coming out of death (water) into his new life. Communion is more difficult to rationalize. The bread represents Christ's physical body broken for us. The blood represents cleansing and total forgiveness. These pictures make a declaration of God drawing you to him and providing everything for your future.

CHAPTER 7

TRAINING

During World War II, Doyle Brown flew missions with the United States armed forces against the Nazi regime in Europe. He was part of the aircrew of a B-24 Liberator bomber. He was the tail gunner in that crew. He didn't just walk to his spot on the aircraft; he had to crawl through the framework of the fuselage to take up his post. The rear gunner was unlike any other member of the flight crew because he spent most of the mission time at the rear of the airplane. He didn't have the same personal interaction with others on board because he was totally isolated. It was an extremely dangerous job. It was the most annoying place to be on a long flight. The noise was horrendous. Most enemy attacks against the bombers originated as fighter planes snuck up from behind hoping to catch the gunner by surprise. The enemy would first shoot at the rear gun turret. Often the returning bomber crews would face a tragic scene as their friend was hosed out of the back of the plane because he had literally been riddled to pieces by machine-gun fire.

Doyle survived. He flew many missions. Through that perilous season of his life, he developed a deep and abiding relationship with God. He lived with the realization that he was the eyes for the whole plane. Their safety and his depended upon him doing a perfect job. The pressure was enormous. If he failed, he wouldn't have lived to make any excuse.

After the war ended, he returned to live in Corpus Christi, Texas, a city where there was a naval base. At the completion of the Pacific and European campaigns, the city emptied because many of the people had been affiliated with the war effort. Doyle found himself having to decide. Should he return to Houston or make a go of what would develop in Corpus Christi? It must have been a brave decision to make, but maybe his courage and foresight had been shaped through challenging war missions. Numerous low-cost houses had been built during the war to house military families, and many of these had become vacant. The cost of these local houses was low, and so was optimism.

Doyle had survived the war because God helped him in a variety of ways. He had been trained through the experience to see beyond his own immediate circumstances. His mind was trained to think about what was out there. What were the possibilities? He ended up with a different perspective from that of many people.

Doyle was a left-handed sign painter. The challenge that lefties have is that they can't easily use a common mahl stick to rest their hand on while they do their lettering (many write from right to left to solve the problem). Doyle dispensed with the idea of using a stick or resting on his little finger. He would stick out his left hand, steady as a rock, and paint beautiful letters left to right. His work was amazing; he was a true artisan of the sign craft world. He created a business in Corpus doing special-event displays and sign work. He learned how to decorate all sorts of theatre backdrops. Any opportunities that he could see usually interested him.

At the same time, many Mexican people were moving into the region hoping to find work. The locals were unimpressed. It was also quite hard for these folks to find accommodation because real estate people were unlikely to rent houses to them. Doyle didn't see these people as a threat or as the enemy. Local people became his friends. He started buying cheap houses and renting them out.

Doyle had style. He was the epitome of a gentleman, but he was also an entrepreneur. His business grew because he not only took risks and worked hard, but also God was obviously helping him. Somewhere in the mix he became a Methodist preacher. Doyle was so kind to me. I was an outsider. A foreigner. I was a young Australian sign painter with not too much experience. There were quite a few people working in his organization called Arrow Display, and somehow, he took me under his guiding wing. I have no idea why, but he placed a whole lot of trust in my abilities. He took me out to extremely difficult projects, and with a very brief introduction, would leave me to work my way through all sorts of different sign painting projects. I remember one project was to paint a business name. This involved drawing and painting five-foot-tall letters down the side of a factory. The artwork must have been a hundred meters long. I had never done anything like that in my life. Doyle supplied a hand-drawn sketch and left me to figure it out. He was a brave man. Every project was challenging. I think he gave me everything that required a great deal of courage. This also included gold leaf gilding on glass doors. Doyle had been a tail gunner. He could see possibilities. He could see what people would become. He was easily my all-time favorite boss.

When I left my employment with Doyle to start my own business in Jacksonville, Arkansas, I modeled every business principle I could from him. I had been trained by Doyle Brown. I hadn't just worked for him; I had gleaned everything I could from my experience with him. Even the smallest detail was important to me—how he treated people and how he worked within the community. Everything helped me. I joined the Chamber of Commerce because that's what Doyle did. I joined the church because that seemed to be important. I had been trained by someone. Training isn't simply taking a course of studies. It's not about getting a degree or a certificate. Training is about learning something that you apply to your life. I think I'm more passionate about training than I am about education. There may be educational processes, but training is not just about information.

The work of the Holy Spirit is not just informational; it is transformational because it trains us to commit to his way of doing what he has taught us. The following is a story of Jesus with his disciples. It displays how God speaks into our lives and how we are likely to respond.

> When Jesus came to the region of Caesarea Philippi, he asked his disciples, "Who do people say the Son of Man is?"
>
> They replied, "Some say John the Baptist; others say Elijah; and still others, Jeremiah or one of the prophets."
>
> "But what about you?" he asked. "Who do you say I am?"
>
> Simon Peter answered, "You are the Messiah, the Son of the living God." (Matthew 16:13–16)

What a huge moment for Peter. Jesus told the group that what he said was not simply speculative but a revelation from God. Peter would have been very excited about having his moment to shine. It was also a monumental conversation and realization for all the disciples. Peter had been running around with Jesus and all his mates, and he lit up with the most profound thought that they were walking with God. Jesus continued with his confirmation of Peter and how he would see the church built upon what was disclosed. Peter swelled with pride. Later that day Peter said something totally messed up.

From that time on Jesus began to explain to his disciples that he must go to Jerusalem and suffer many things at the hands of the elders, the chief priests and the teachers of the law, and that he must be killed and on the third day be raised to life. Peter took him aside and began to rebuke him. "Never, Lord!" he said. "This shall never happen to you!"

Jesus turned and said to Peter, "Get behind me, Satan! You are a stumbling-block to me; you do not have in mind the concerns of God, but merely human concerns." (Matthew 16:21–23)

Jesus shared that various people were going to violently take his life and then, somehow, he was to be raised back to life. Peter was really upset with what Jesus said, and he took Jesus aside to straighten him out. Big mistake! In the previous section, Peter was elated by Jesus's response. However, this response was a reprimand. It couldn't have been any stronger. This was a hit on Peter's ego. Jesus "pulled the carpet" out from under Peter and, in an instant, he fell to the ground. Peter was smashed.

In our own lives we must realize that we will get some things so right, but then in a heartbeat, we can get so much wrong. I get things wrong on so many occasions. I would prefer to preach a message to 10,000 people than to be at a church business meeting with thirty people. It's so easy to become defensive when dealing with policies and constitutions. I never feel defensive when I'm preaching the gospel. I don't always say the things I need to say the way I need to say them. The same will be true for you. The question is, whom do you listen too? Is it God? Or are we caught up with our own ideas about how things will work out?

Jesus was referring to the teachers of religion in his day. They were messed up completely. They were concerned about all sorts of things, and they totally missed the significance of who Jesus was. The minute we think we know more than Jesus, we have a massive problem. You might say that you don't have problems. Think about when Jesus said, "Don't worry." How many people have conquered this? We all worry from time to time. Think about how we judge people or how well we care for marginalized people. None of us has the right to judge or refuse to care. How many of us love our neighbors? Do we even know their names? We all have an amazing ability to do extraordinary things with our lives, but equally we can get much wrong. How does God help us along the journey? The question goes back to whom do you listen to?

> Watch out for false prophets. They come to you in sheep's clothing, but inwardly they are ferocious wolves. By their fruit you will recognize them. Do people pick grapes from thorn-bushes, or figs from thistles? Likewise, every good tree bears good fruit, but a bad tree bears bad fruit. A good tree cannot bear bad fruit, and a bad tree cannot bear good fruit. Every tree that does not bear good fruit is cut down and thrown into

the fire. Thus, by their fruit you will recognize them. (Matthew 7:15–20)

What kind of person would you listen too? I'm likely to listen to someone like Doyle Brown. I was trained by him to do all sorts of things. Throughout your life you will find that you listen to different people at different times. Some people will play significant roles in your life. You want to look toward those who have the principles of Jesus in their lives; otherwise, you will get ahead of yourself. Jesus talked about false prophets. How do you recognize a false prophet? How wrong does a prophet have to be before he or she is deemed false? How can you tell? Jesus talked about the people who thought they were doing the right thing by God, but they were not. They wanted to take Jesus out of the story. Watch out for those people who say they are doing the right thing, but you know they are not. Peter said to Jesus that nothing bad could happen to him. Peter had to be corrected.

It is by their lives that you know if they are producing what is right. That is important for us. Today, if we are uncertain about something, we go to Google looking for answers. The problem we have is that we don't know anything about the people who are supplying the answers. Jesus was really concerned that people would have the ability to observe someone's life. Jesus was sent to Earth to physically connect with people. God didn't do a remote televised edition of what he wanted to say. He sent himself as a representative. Jesus "did" life with his disciples. Who are you doing life with? Jesus modeled this style of ministry.

Therefore, everyone who hears these words of mine and puts them into practice is like a wise man who built his house on the rock. The rain

came down, the streams rose, and the winds
blew and beat against that house; yet it did not
fall, because it had its foundation on the rock.
But everyone who hears these words of mine
and does not put them into practice is like a
foolish man who built his house on sand. The
rain came down, the streams rose, and the
winds blew and beat against that house, and it
fell with a great crash.' When Jesus had finished
saying these things, the crowds were amazed at
his teaching, because he taught as one who had
authority, and not as their teachers of the law.
(Matthew 24–29)

This is not about building a house. This is about living out
the right kind of life. I don't find it easy to be patient. What
does he mean to carefully build our lives on him? These are the
words of Jesus. He is the one we are supposed to be listening
to. What he says has got to come into our lives. There's no point
in making up our own standards; they won't hold up. It's the
work of the Holy Spirit to reveal things to us. He is training us
to put the words of Jesus into our everyday lives. If we do this
long enough, we will experience the benefits. The Holy Spirit
is a person. You can grieve the Holy Spirit. You can quench the
Holy Spirit. The Holy Spirit is not automatic. He is a person. He
influences our lives. We grow to become receptive of his work.
When Doyle was flying missions over Europe, he had no one to
protect him. He relied on God. He was drawn deeper into God.
It was God's Spirit that got Doyle home. Doyle was trained by
the Holy Spirit. He used the insight and the skill that he had.
The planes swooped down out of the sky, and he had to dig
deep in the moment to hope he was up to the task that he had

before him. He experienced ferocious enemy attacks. Training is not just information. Training enables us to fly well.

I do PowerPoint presentations. Often, I use a black background with white writing. Most people might think I simply prefer this combination, but it's more than that. In my sign training, I learned that, when readers are presented with black letters on a white background, they read the background. The reasoning is quite simple: all light is emitted from white, and no light comes from black. If you use white letters on black, people read the letters. It is supposed to stimulate a better optical experience. Some people might say, "I don't believe that!" I would have to shrug my shoulders and hang my head because I realize I don't have a PowerPoint disciple; I have an unbeliever. I learned this fact somewhere. It makes sense to me, so I apply it to my work. There is no point in learning something and then ignoring logic or good science in the principle. In applying the knowledge to my work, I reap the benefits of knowing I'm doing what I learned. That is effective training.

Let's go back to Jesus. He said not to worry. How many of us practice it? The truth is that we must apply what we know over our lifetimes to see lasting benefits.

Doyle Brown was the best boss I ever had. It was pointless to learn principles from Doyle if I wasn't going to apply them to my life. I left Corpus Christi to start my own business in Jacksonville, Arkansas. In Jacksonville, I did what I had seen Doyle do. I joined the Chamber of Commerce. I went to church. I copied his business methods. I learned from Doyle. It was good training because it worked. I saw good fruit.

When I went to Bible college years later, I learned something interesting. There are many people who go into Bible training with their own distinct beliefs. They usually come out of college with the same distinctives that they held before they went in.

They didn't go there to be trained as much as they went there because it was a requirement. They had their view of God, and it never changed. I learned that in college. The students shared that fact. I was in disbelief because I was the opposite. I needed to be trained. I was hungry. I loved going to my lectures. Those lecturers had put runs on the board. They had lived lives that had produced fruit. I gleaned all sorts of understanding from simply taking in everything that I could.

Recently, my daughter felt the need to pray for me. She went to my wife and asked her to join her in prayer. It was a lovely time of prayer. I was moved. In the moment, I realized that she was a young lady who had been trained to bear fruit. I knew she understood the importance of not only praying, but putting into practice prayers for others.

Jesus amazed the crowd because he was one who had authority. He wasn't like the religious teachers of the day. He preached the word like no one else. The people were blessed by him. The Holy Spirit will be your teacher. He will drive home the words of Jesus into your life. "Don't worry" becomes a reality of blessing when we apply this principle and many others into our lives.

We must take an active interest in spiritual training.

> Do not conform to the pattern of this world, but
> be transformed by the renewing of your mind.
> Then you will be able to test and approve what
> God's will is—his good, pleasing and perfect
> will. (Romans 12:2)

If we keep thinking the same way we think today, and we never develop a new way of seeing what God wants us to see, we miss what he is showing us. We all want to know what God expects out of us, but if we keep following the same old ways, we will get the same old results. The Holy Spirit must have the ability to shape us. He might, occasionally, say that I've said some great things, but at other times, he is going to rebuke me. He might say, "Where on earth did you get that from?" This is important because we invite God to talk into our minds.

Paul the Apostle wrote words to Timothy who was his apprentice: "What you heard from me, keep as the pattern of sound teaching, with faith and love in Christ Jesus. Guard the good deposit that was entrusted to you—guard it with the help of the Holy Spirit who lives in us" (2 Timothy 1:13–14).

If you save a dollar a week, you'll accumulate $52 by the end of a year. Accumulating that money gives you power. In the same way, applying whatever Paul taught Timothy was important. He wasn't alone in doing this. He could guard it with the help of the Holy Spirit. It would end up paying dividends.

We might have deficiencies with patience. Jesus is trustworthy. What he says works. We need the training if we want to experience what his teaching is all about. The benefits come to those who practice what Jesus says: "May the God of hope fill you with all joy and peace as you trust in him, so that you may overflow with hope by the power of the Holy Spirit" (Romans 15:13).

CHAPTER 8

RELOCATION

We live in an age of increasing mobility. People can move to many parts of the world and live there. It's awesome. I am Australian. I was born in Australia and raised in Papua New Guinea. I've had careers in both countries, and I've had two periods of residency in the United States of America. I'm not the only one who has moved around. Many people have done so, and many more will find this is a common practice in life. Perhaps it always has been, but now we have almost an ease of ability to move around and to relocate in a different way.

Recently I was chatting with several people who had been made redundant in their various vocations and were processing changes in their lives. Even these people are essentially being relocated, even if they are not moving in a geographical sense. People are migrating from war-torn countries. Others are leaving families for a variety of reasons. People are on the move. It's a big part of our lives. These moves can be the most challenging times in our lives.

While the Bible is filled with people being relocated for one reason or another, one person who really stands out is Joseph. He didn't willingly move on. Joseph found himself in a family separated by rifts. His father, Jacob (also named Israel), had three wives. I'm sure that created dramas. But think about families today. I know many wonderful people who come from families that have a variety of moms and dads. So, the story fits well. Joseph was a teenager and somehow got to oversee the work that his older brothers were doing. In that role, he managed to tell his father that the brothers were not doing what they ought to be doing. This infuriated the brothers, and they became jealous of Joseph. Jacob gave Joseph an ornate coat to wear. It must have been very beautiful, and that gift drove a wedge between Joseph and his brothers. In some ways, they must have felt as if they had been rejected by their dad. Joseph may have been naïve or a bit brash, but he told the brothers about a dream he'd had in which one day they bowed down to him. It was a rash thing to tell the brothers, and they didn't take it well. They became irate with jealousy. And to make matters worse, he told them another dream in which even their parents bowed down to him, and that got him into far worse trouble. Jacob was upset by the dream, and the brothers hated Joseph because of his dreams.

The relocation of Joseph came about because Joseph had been sent to check up on his brothers out in the fields. They were tending the sheep. When they saw him coming down the path, they plotted to kill him. They didn't end up killing him, but they did rip his coat from him and throw him down a dry well. When some Arab traders came by, they pulled him up and sold him to them as a slave. They relocated Joseph to Egypt. The brothers took the coat back to Jacob covered in blood. They told him a fabricated story about wild animals attacking and killing Joseph. Jacob was devastated.

It is an awful story, but the principles are there. Jacob was a deceiver in his younger life when he usurped his own brother's birthright. In the story we see that the brothers imitated the father with made-up stories to cover their deeds. In so many people's lives, there are instances of sinful behavior that precipitate moves to new jobs, new countries, and into pioneering ventures. There is no such thing as a perfect life in this broken world, but somehow, God works in all sorts of ways to bring about ultimate good.

You may or may not have had a dream about future aspects of your life. I've had several memorable dreams that haven't made much sense, but I've experienced many instances when good ideas sure seemed to be God inspired. People talk about vision. Vision is important because it paints a picture of what the future might look like. I think it is true that God will communicate specific aspects of his desires for your life to you. You will know because you know. There will be a uniqueness in your story. Usually there is a seed planted in your heart that doesn't go away. It begins to grow or at least always remains in your thoughts. Not everyone will understand your dreams, and sometimes it's a good idea to be careful about whom you tell your future aspirations to.

The Spirit of God uses whatever he likes to give us a glimpse into what lies ahead in our lives.

> In the last days, God says, I will pour out my Spirit on all people. Your sons and daughters will prophesy, your young men will see visions, your old men will dream dreams. Even on my servants, both men and women, I will pour out my Spirit in those days, and they will prophesy. (Acts 2:17–18)

There isn't a formula for God's Spirit in your life. The Holy Spirit is a person, and he will bring about what he intends to bring about through you. God may have revealed a dream to Joseph, but he didn't give him an interpretation of exactly what was to take place. If he had sent a prophet to Joseph with exact details, Joseph might have told the prophet that he must be talking to the wrong brother. It's the same in our lives; we are not likely to know very much at all. But we may get to see an important aspect of what lies ahead.

Joseph never thought that he would have career opportunities in Egypt. He was relocated there because God had plans, and God used even the most messed-up scenarios to bring about exactly what he wanted.

Joseph became a slave in Egypt. Potiphar was the captain of the guard of the pharaoh in Egypt. He purchased Joseph and gave him a job working at his home. Joseph did a terrific job, and God enabled him to be a real standout in the house. Potiphar's wife must have had way too much time on her hands, and she was attracted to the handsome young Hebrew. She wanted to have a sexual affair with him, and she went after him every day. Joseph resisted every advance that she made. He rejected her advances. Finally, one day, she cornered him in her room, grabbed hold of his robe, and pulled his clothes off. He sprinted away, and she fabricated a story to her husband about how Joseph was trying to seduce her or perhaps even rape her. Potiphar believed his wife. He was shocked by what he heard, and he sent Joseph to prison. In some ways, Joseph was relocated twice. Talk about a bad run.

I can't help but think that the Spirit of God uses dissatisfaction to move us on. Joseph's brothers were dissatisfied with how their father saw them. It caused a great deal of jealousy and hatred in the family. God also used the dissatisfaction of Potiphar's wife to move Joseph on. She was probably used to getting her own way, but through rejection, she created a scene that caused the dismissal and removal of Joseph from her house. Joseph lost his family, his country, and his job. He ended up in prison.

You might be doing everything right in your life or your job or in your family; however, an upheaval of your life is still possible because other people may be jealous of who you are. What seems to happen is that the proverbial rug can be pulled out from under you. You may question why things go down the way they do, and you may even question why God allows bad things to happen to you.

You would think that God would have kept Joseph out of prison. He didn't. Through imprisonment, Joseph met the Pharaoh and fulfilled his dream. Sometimes it is the holding places that become our darkest times; they may result in the most spiritual moments in our lives.

Joseph met two people in prison who had significant dreams. One was the baker, who died as Joseph predicted, and the other was the cup bearer to the Pharaoh. Joseph interpreted his dream with a favorable outcome and asked the cup bearer to put a good word in for him when he got out of prison. Joseph remained in prison. The cup bearer got his job back and totally neglected Joseph in prison. Life can be a bit like that. You help someone. You do the right thing by him, but for one reason or another, he carries on with his life, and your needs go unmet. God uses hardships to strengthen your faith for what comes next in your life. In our toughest situations, God does his deepest work in us.

While often our relocations may very well be planned, other times that is not the case. We end up in a variety of different situations that could have or should have worked out well, but they don't. You might well be asking, "Why am I here?" C. S. Lewis wrote, "You are never too old to set another goal or dream a new dream." People want to know there is something that is good ahead for them. I can deal with prayers being answered with a "yes." I'm not so fond of are "no" answers. I really struggle when God demands that I wait. That is torture. It's like being in a prison. Maybe I'm being a bit dramatic. But I'm not so patient. I'm ready for my big break *now*. Our relocations are marked with periods of waiting. I often think about the remarkable outlook that Paul the Apostle had when he was in prison. Paul wrote, "Rejoice in the Lord always, and again I say, rejoice" (Philippians 4:4). Why did he write such a thing? He was in prison and going nowhere. It's not as if he had anything to sing about. No! He wrote that because he knew there were people to encourage and that he needed gratitude in his heart. Otherwise he would find himself withdrawn into a place that he didn't need to go to. None of us needs to go there.

Several years after his incarceration, Joseph got his big break. The Pharaoh had a bizarre dream and needed someone to tell him what it was all about. The cup bearer suddenly remembered Joseph. (Let's hope this was the case, and he hadn't purposely ignored his former prison mate.) Joseph heard the dream and diagnosed the meaning. Additionally, he advised a course of action for Egypt. It turns out that the entire region was going to experience seven good and prosperous years due to an increase in rainfall, and then seven perilous years because of a severe drought. Joseph's plan was to conserve all the grain and food resources for seven years so that they would have enough food for the next seven years. The insight was spot-on. The plan was an effective strategy to help the Egyptian people survive. The pharaoh recruited Joseph in a heartbeat. God moved Joseph into his dream job. He became the second in command of all Egypt. His new role was overseeing the distribution of grain.

Meanwhile, back in Canaan, drought had set in, and the family of Jacob ran short of food. Joseph's brothers were sent to Egypt to source food.

Joseph's original dream came to fulfillment. Can you imagine the emotional drama that Joseph experienced when he saw his brothers bowing before him begging to buy grain from him? Remember his brothers had rejected him; they had almost killed him! They had sold him. They hated him. They were super jealous of him. They had devised the scheme to get rid of him by selling him to traders as a slave. In an instant, his whole life appeared before him. He recognized them, but his brothers had no idea that they were bowing down to their brother. Joseph couldn't handle what he felt. He had to leave them and go into another room and weep, and not just a few tears. He cried his eyes out because it was a moment in time for which he had never prepared himself. All sorts of emotions swept over him.

His encounters with his brothers went on for some time, and he had made various requests of them, but he processed his hurts extremely well. Finally, he told them who he was. He had been totally messed up in the ordeal, but somehow, he managed to get his head around why things had gone down the way they had.

> Then Joseph said to his brothers, "Come close to me." When they had done so, he said, "I am your brother Joseph, the one you sold into Egypt! And now, do not be distressed and do not be angry with yourselves for selling me here, because it was to save lives that God sent me ahead of you. For two years now there has been famine in the land, and for the next five years there will be no ploughing and reaping. But God sent me ahead of you to preserve for you a remnant on Earth

and to save your lives by a great deliverance."
(Genesis 45:5-7)

Joseph realized that the vision he'd had hadn't indicated that he was going to be great. The dream was all about how God was going to bring to fruition his great plan for the family of Israel. It was about salvation. We can all learn something from this. Many of us have dreams about our lives, but what we might never know is how God is going to impact generations to come. God's overarching narrative is one of redemption. God is calling people to himself in a personal relationship of salvation through Jesus Christ. You get to share in that vision. You get a piece of his dream.

The Spirit of God moves us into his place his way, in his season, and for his purposes. It's not as if you can map out your every step in your life. If you could do that, you wouldn't need a savior. If you could figure out your career moves, you wouldn't need God. The truth is, we can't figure out so much in life. We live with the dynamic of faith. Faith evaluates our next step through his leading. God gives us his revelation at the right time so that things unfold the way he wants them to. We must keep in mind that he has things together even when we don't.

If we get drawn into "it's all about me," we lose our perspective. We take our eyes off Jesus. How do I put my gaze back where it belongs? Jesus offers salvation. There is also the prophesized return of Christ one day. There will one day be a time of no more tears, no more brokenness. All things will be the way they ought to be. In the meanwhile, we need to maintain our sensitivities toward the work of the Holy Spirit. We need reminders that we are children of God. We are part of a family that is drawn into his goodness. You are a child much loved by your Father who is in heaven.

CHAPTER 9

RESOURCES

Bill Hayden is the former governor general of Australia. He spent much of his life claiming to be an atheist. Recently, he changed. It was reported by one of the newspapers that he went through a health crisis of sorts and met a Christian person who helped him see God through her actions. There would have been a time when he would have rejected any sort of spiritual dialogue, but he found himself wanting to encourage Australians to discover faith in Jesus Christ. This happened to Bill when he was in his eighties. A genuine conversion can happen at any time of our lives.

There is a cartoon that shows a group of people in a lifeboat. In the background is a sinking ship. In the life boat, one character is the captain and another is Elvis. Elvis is standing up, and the caption reads, "Don't go rocking the boat." Obviously, it's a bit of a dad joke, but it's quite good. A creative would recognize that the captain is telling Elvis to sit down because he could upset the craft and they would all end up in the water. My thought was that, if the captain was doing such a good job, why was the ship sinking? Elvis wanted to do what he knew how to do. He wanted to entertain the sad occupants in the lifeboat. Although there are hordes of Elvis impersonators around the world, the truth is that there was only ever one Elvis Presley. If that Elvis stood up in your life boat, you would be thrilled to be serenaded by him. More than likely, he would end up being the highlight of an otherwise awful cruise. Elvis was a one of a kind. He was an original, and no one can replace him. In that same way of thinking, there can only ever be one you. You are an original. It's only when you care to stand up in the right moments that people will be blessed because you are who you are. There will always be some pompous, self-righteous, judgmental characters wanting you to bury your talent. However, if you look at them closely enough, you will recognize more about them and why they want to silence you. When our lives on Earth come to an end, we want to know that we have lived out good lives. Each of us wants to hear from the master himself, "Well done, good and faithful servant" (Matthew 25:21). To hear these words ring out, you must be a person who uses what God has entrusted you with. You want to know that you have done a good job.

In my life, I have probably hired or been the boss of several hundred people. Most of the time I've worked in creative fields as well as serving as a senior pastor in two churches. Creative people are different—sometimes really different. Creative people are often the most sensitive to work with. There is a reason for that. The more creative they are, the more sensitive they are likely to be. This may not always be apparent, but I think it's fairly true. Deeply artistic people have a gift, but in some ways, they live with a bit of a curse. Hard-working people are likely to develop thick skin and be resilient. Creatives have an extraordinary ability to see something beyond normality; they see possibilities. In seeing what doesn't exist, they become the interpreters for the rest of society. It comes at a price. In their gift, they are likely to take things quite personally. They feel what some people can hardly even see. Their perception is at their core of being rather than derived as information. People want to see plans. The artist can visualize what doesn't exist.

When you work with artists in highly stressful environments with challenging deadlines, you encounter unhappy workers who want to resign. They want to quit because they can't handle anything that is perceived to be unreasonable. I found that Friday afternoon was the most popular time of the week for people to offer their resignations. If the person was difficult to work with and not adding value to the organization, I welcomed his or her resignation. However, most of the time the unhappy workers were worth keeping. I would take their notice, but I'd tell them I wasn't going to act on the termination until after the weekend. I would tell them to take Monday off and then let me know on Tuesday if they were still feeling the same way. I think most of those people changed their minds within a few days because they allowed their emotions to grab hold of a better reality and remind themselves that there is no such thing as a perfect job.

We all can get down about our jobs. It happens. Recently I was feeling down about the church in which I served as senior pastor. I shared some of my frustrations with a friend, and that friend gave the following advice: "You need to resign from that church and get another job in another church where they will appreciate you. But when you get to that church, don't rock the boat." I agreed. It sounded like great advice. After about ten minutes, I came to my senses. I realized that I could never go anywhere without rocking the boat. I'm a creative. I see possibilities. I see patterns of behavior that will sink the ship. I can see fantastic ways to spread the good news about Jesus Christ. The problem is that I can't not be myself. Wherever I go, I go. If I stopped rocking the boat, I'd be burying my talent. God has invested his spirit within me for a reason. The same is true for you. You can't not be you and still expect to hear, "Well done, good and faithful servant."

How do we know what God wants us to do? Jesus tells us in a parable:

> Again, it will be like a man going on a journey, who called his servants and entrusted his wealth to them. To one he gave five bags of gold, to another two bags, and to another one bag, each according to his ability. Then he went on his journey. The man who had received five bags of gold went at once and put his money to work and gained five bags more. So also, the one with two bags of gold gained two more. But the man who had received one bag went off, dug a hole in the ground and hid his master's money. After a long time the master of those servants returned and settled accounts with them. The man who had received five bags of gold brought the other five. "Master," he said, "you entrusted me with five bags of gold. See, I have gained five more."
>
> His master replied, "Well done, good and faithful servant! You have been faithful with a few things; I will put you in charge of many things. Come and share your master's happiness!"
>
> The man with two bags of gold also came. "Master," he said, "you entrusted me with two bags of gold: see, I have gained two more."
>
> His master replied, "Well done, good and faithful servant! You have been faithful with a few

things; I will put you in charge of many things. Come and share your master's happiness!"

Then the man who had received one bag of gold came. "Master," he said, "I knew that you are a hard man, harvesting where you have not sown and gathering where you have not scattered seed. So I was afraid and went out and hid your gold in the ground. See, here is what belongs to you."

His master replied, "You wicked, lazy servant! So you knew that I harvest where I have not sown and gather where I have not scattered seed? Well then, you should have put my money on deposit with the bankers, so that when I returned I would have received it back with interest. So, take the bag of gold from him and give it to the one who has ten bags. For whoever has will be given more, and they will have an abundance. Whoever does not have, even what they have will be taken from them. And throw that worthless servant outside, into the darkness, where there will be weeping and gnashing of teeth." (Matthew 25:14–30)

It's too easy to dwell on the negative aspects of this parable. I don't think Jesus was trying to put fear into his disciples. He was telling them that God gives his resources out in accordance with abilities, but he doesn't want us to bury what he gives us just because we are afraid of what is required. He is looking to celebrate with his followers. We learn that we are responsible to use the resources God has given us.

When I was a child in Papua New Guinea, there was a company called Missionary Aviation Fellowship. They were stationed in Wewak on the northern coast. They had lots of different aircraft and flew all over PNG helping missionaries with their activities. Imagine if they decided to ground their planes because it was too dangerous to fly in that country. The planes were the resource. The employees were expected to use them. The planes cost supporters a whole lot of money, and they had a great deal of potential to help further the kingdom of God. However, if the workers buried their resources in fear, they were wasting finances because it would have been better to put their money in the bank and gain interest. While this may seem like an elementary example, the principle is about using what God has provided.

Imagine if you took an ordinary bucket and filled it up with time or talent or treasure. That is what God has given you. He has measured out so much time, talent, or treasure. But take that picture further. God gives knowledge, skills, experience, and even health. You have five bucket loads of "good stuff." The question is, what are you going to do with what he has given you? He gives out so much personality or freedom. See these as valuable resources. What about your position in life? You might be a teacher. That's your bucket. What are you going to do? Bury your gift? No, you are going to develop what God has given you. You use your influence. What about buildings? Your home? What about your church buildings? I have often wondered if churches bury their true potential because their buildings are vacant six out of seven days of the week.

If you use your resources, the resources increase in value. I learned that from this parable of Jesus. Take, for instance, a church that sets aside $5,000 for evangelism. If that money sits in the bank, it doesn't do much. If people in the neighborhood are uninterested in your church, what would happen if you touched them with what they are interested in? Let's buy a coffee cart and start selling coffee to stay-at-home parents. In a year, you might have ten families coming to visit your church. Those families would get to know you. They would begin to have significant and meaningful conversations with you. They would start attending a service here and there. Bill Hayden, the governor general of Australia, was in his eighties when he saw Jesus in another person who was kind to him. What if elderly people began to take an interest in the church? This is a principle that Jesus started. Use your resources; by using them, the resources increase in value. Doing nothing with your buildings or money is like burying what God has given you.

And then, the value of what you do multiplies. Let's look at a golfing analogy. If you want to drive a ball from the tee to the hole, you start with a wood and give the ball a good "whack" down the fairway. Very rarely do you get a hole in one. You must take quite a few shots to get the ball in the hole. (If I were playing golf, it would take more shots than I care to admit.) When it comes to evangelism, help move someone from where they are to where they need to be. It might take a few movements, a few off-course efforts, a sand wedge chipped in for good measure, and putting around a green for more time that we should. The coffee shop is like a wood. It's not likely to drive home a hole in one, but it will add value in the process of moving someone from unbelief toward eventual faith. The more people being moved off the tee, the greater the value multiplies.

If you want to understand the leading of the Holy Spirit in all of this, consider that the local church works through the interplay of gifts. Everything God has distributed, according to his judgement of our abilities, must be used. There is no point hiding what God has bestowed upon you. There is no time to question whether God is going to treat you right. There is an evolution of reality taking place. Our local environments are constantly changing. The various generations are very different. What one person values or emphasizes does not match the way others are motivated or moved. We must connect with the ball, not keep taking air swings. The gifts are changing expressions with all sorts of different emphasis being added. Some people are still talking about the good old days. But their children are uninterested in their religion. The church works through what God gives, so we should receive. We receive his word into our hearts. However, we are meant to give out or use what he has given us. God provides people with resources. The Holy Spirit gives good gifts. Those gifts are to be used. What is the point of burying your gift of encouragement? You might have a teaching gift or a helping gift. Whatever you do, don't let anyone discourage you from taking a stand and using your unique resource.

Chapter 10

Courage

Anne Cary is an Australian nurse who recently won the [Florence] Nightingale Award for Excellence in Nursing. Anne is a lady who lives to show kindness to people. When the Ebola crisis erupted in West Africa, many countries from around the world sent their representatives to combat the deadly virus. Anne heard the call to go and tackle the problem head on. She visited a few people in Australia to prepare for her mission against Ebola. Essentially, she bid her partner a forever farewell before she flew off for Sierra Leone. She thought she might contract the disease and die. She was an outsider. A foreigner. On her arrival, someone thrust a baby into her arms who was gravely ill with Ebola. She nursed that child for several hours right up until its death. That was her welcome into what was to unfold for her.

There were many patients at the camp hospital, and Anne, dressed in what resembled a moon-walking suit, tried to treat as many people as possible. She often felt that all she could offer them was kindness before they slipped into eternity. It was a terrible disease, and it was ripping apart families. The mother who met her at the airport had lost seven children and her husband to the onslaught of Ebola. Anne couldn't physically touch anyone, but they could see her eyes, and those eyes told a story of deep compassion. Each day she had to decommission the moon-suit by going through a chlorinated wash. That wash was essential for the safety of Anne as well as her entire team. She praised the contributions of her team and certainly did not single herself out for significant recognition.

On returning to Australia, she was heralded as a hero; however, she reported that she didn't feel much like a hero. Yes, she may have had heroic moments, but she didn't see herself in any special light. Instead, she said that the real heroes were the people who willingly came forward at the clinic declaring that they were infected with Ebola. The medical teams from around the world not only tackled the problem, they also defeated its death hold on people. The reason they were successful in the campaign against Ebola was that they were able to learn about the virus as they examined and treated patients. As many people died, others benefitted from what members of the medical profession learned from those who died in the process.

In Christianity, success happens only when people willingly come forward knowing they have been infected by sin. Sin carries a death sentence. Oddly enough, these people (we) become the heroes. Through our testimonies, others identify with what we share with them, and they can also recognize where they presently are at spiritually. Instead of Anne, Jesus Christ is the sent savior ready to administer his saving grace. People who hide or deny the "sickness" miss out on what God is willing to freely give. Jesus offers water to those who are thirsty. In a spiritual sense, this is what we humans lack. We require forgiveness for our sins and a spiritual journey forward led by God. God has been on a mission since the beginning of time to redeem people. Daniel says God rescues and he saves (Daniel 6:5).

In 605 BCE, King Nebuchadnezzar of Babylon conquered the city of Jerusalem and took captives to Babylon. The period of exile from Jerusalem officially lasted seventy years. In that time, the Persians took control of Babylon, including the Jewish people living in exile. In around 522 BCE, Daniel, a Jewish exile, was given a prominent leadership role in the new Persian kingdom of King Darius. Daniel was an outsider. He was a foreigner. He didn't belong in Babylon, but he ended up living there. Darius governed quite well through a system of satraps (governors). Daniel excelled in one of those roles until the king singled him out to lead the whole nation. That promotion caused a great deal of jealousy.

The Persian leaders tried to incriminate Daniel with some sort of moral scandal from his past, but it seemed that Daniel was a model citizen in Babylon. They concocted a plan to trick the king into removing Daniel. They went to him, appealing to his ego. They got him to sign a thirty-day law into effect that anyone caught praying to a god or a mortal other than the king was to be thrown into a den filled with hungry lions. It was a death sentence. The king signed the order and, by doing so, put in place the edict that was aimed at flushing out Daniel. Daniel learned about the new law. His practice was to pray three times a day toward Jerusalem. He kept doing what he had always done. He kept praying three times a day. The other leaders, who were jealous of Daniel, made sure they caught him in the act. It turns out that he prayed next to an open window, so it was easy for his enemies to catch him at it.

The jealous leaders informed on Daniel. The king recognized that Daniel was brilliant at his job and that he had a genuine relationship with the real God. At first, he was taken aback and tried to work out how to exclude Daniel from the punishment that was attached to the law. After a day, he succumbed to enact the law that he had signed into effect. He ordered that Daniel be thrown into the den of lions. He placed his stamp of approval on the process with a belief that God would rescue Daniel and save him from death.

It was an awful night for the king, and I'm sure Daniel was terrified as well, surrounded as he was by lions. At daybreak, the king went to the den and called out to Daniel asking him if he was alive. Daniel called back to the king and told him that God had sent an angel to close the mouths of the lions. The angel was the servant of God. It was a joyous occasion for the king to be reunited with Daniel and to set him free.

The outcome of this story wasn't so good for the conniving leaders and their families. They had planned Daniel's death, and so the king repaid them with the same sentence. He threw them all into the lion's den, and of course the lions devoured them.

When we look at our spiritual journey with God, we need to look at where we are and, more specifically, we need to look at our families. If you have children or grandchildren, where are they in their spiritual lives? Are they adopting your religious traditions? Maybe they are totally uninterested in your faith. Or they may have their own convictions that determine what they believe and how they live out their lives. This is important because it will reflect your true impact on others, or more correctly, the fruit of your journey. We know that God is with us every day and that he helps us. God is on a redemptive mission. In our families, God is at work. We praise God because he has redeemed us. We have a victory in Jesus. This victory will transfer into our families if we are willing to come forward and share how we have been saved. We know that sin is a factor, and religious practices don't resolve sin. God alone rescues and saves us from sin, and it is by his grace that we experience his redemption.

Daniel was brave. He was courageous. He was amazing in his work, but it was his personal relationship with God that gave him the courage to continue living out his faith. It was his personal convictions that enabled him to continue convening with God even when the law said he must not do so. Daniel defied the law. However, he was exonerated by God through forgiveness. He was free of all charges. He was also rescued from certain death. We need the courage that Daniel displayed—courage not so much to be a hero, but courage to acknowledge our sins and courage to live out our convictions.

There are many examples of people who lived through moments when they had to be brave. I call these "Babylon moments." Take, for example, Noah. Noah was a righteous man. He did all the right things when no one seemed to do what was right. In his society, he didn't fit in. He wasn't part of the popular crowd. God asked him to begin a ridiculously crazy project. He recruited Noah to build the massive watertight box large enough to carry one pair of every animal. That was way beyond reasonable. Noah did it. That's the crazy part. He gathered all the materials together and set about building an ark. Can you imagine the flak he received from his neighbors? The very basis of Noah's mission was redemption. God rescued and saved not only the animals, but also Noah's family. God could have built the boat himself, but he chose to put Noah to work with a huge project. Noah was courageous—not perfect, but certainly courageous in his task.

What about Miriam? She was an outsider, a foreigner in Egypt. Miriam was Moses' sister. Moses was born to be a savior of sorts. His job was to get the Israelite slaves out of Egypt. He was born in a terrible age when Hebrew baby boys were slaughtered. God chose a deliverer for the Hebrew people. To save her son, Moses' mother placed him in a reed basket and set him among the reeds of the Nile river. Pharaohs' wife discovered him. Miriam risked her life to aid the Egyptian party that found him. That act was brave. She was courageous. God didn't need Miriam, but he chose to use her in a brave moment. She had her faults.

There is also the story of Gideon. The Israelite people were living in the Promised Land, but they did so in great fear. They lived like outsiders. It was a Babylon of sorts. They were being oppressed by the Midianite people. Gideon was an insignificant man from an insignificant family in an insignificant tribe. He was scared for his life. God met him in a pit designed to be a wine press. He was threshing wheat hoping no one saw him. An angel appeared to him and requested that he save his people. He was taken completely by surprise at the assigned task and certainly wanted God to prove to him in no uncertain terms that he was indeed the designated "savior." God made Gideon cull the army down to three hundred men, and then he gave him a ludicrous order to destroy thousands of enemies. Gideon did it. I'm sure he was shaking in his sandals, but he did what God asked him to do, and he was victorious. God was with him every step of the way. Oh, Gideon was like you and me. He tested God to make sure he really was hearing from God.

Ruth is another example of a courageous person. Naomi had moved with her husband and two sons to Moab. The men died. Ruth, who was from Moab, had married one of the sons. When Naomi returned to live near Jerusalem at Bethlehem, Ruth tagged along with her own faith in God. She may have had faith in their God, but she was a foreigner, an outsider, and a woman in a male-dominated culture. Her money-making opportunities were woeful. She found herself as not much more than a beggar at a foreign farm. However, God used her in his redemptive saga. She ended up marrying Boaz, and in doing so had children with direct lineage to King David and to Jesus Christ. Ruth was courageous to follow Naomi home, and she had to have courageous moments connecting with Boaz.

Perhaps one of the greatest stories of courage is the story of Mary, the mother of Jesus. Mary had never had sex, but she found herself pregnant by God. She was chosen to be the mother of the child who was going to save the world from sin. Can you imagine eyebrows being raised? People would have said all sorts of things about her. Everyone would have jumped on the gossip vine. Mary wasn't from Bethlehem. Joseph, her betrothed, took her there. She was an outsider. When it came time for her to deliver the baby, there was no room in any of the inns. She was about to deliver the King of Kings, and God didn't manipulate things so that she was comfortable. She delivered the baby in an animal pen to fulfil his scriptures. Don't tell me that act didn't require a whole lot of courage. Her whole life demanded huge moments of courage.

Peter the disciple was impetuous, but he was also courageous. He was from the region of Galilee. He was an outsider to the city of Jerusalem. He wasn't a member of one of the religious sects. He had chosen to follow Jesus. On the night that Jesus was arrested in the garden of Gethsemane outside the walls of the city, Peter cut the ear off one of the arresting people. Whack! It happened in an instant. Peter was going to fight the fight of his life to save his master. Understand, I'm more impressed with Peter's act of courage than Jesus ever was. Jesus resorted to rescuing the bloodied ear from the dust and restoring it to its rightful place on the servant's head. Nevertheless, Peter was very brave. Don't forget that, other than Jesus, he is the only one who managed to walk on water.

The Apostle Paul was brave on many occasions. He lived a courageous life. He was imprisoned, flogged, beaten, and shipwrecked, but he lived knowing that his life's mission was to work for the redemption of others. One time at Galatia, Peter and Barnabas were drawn into the Jewish error of linking traditions with the gospel requirements. They both tried to fit in with the religious thinking of the day rather than live by gospel convictions of freedom in Christ. It was a huge mistake. It became their Babylon, but they blew it. Paul stood up to both men and corrected them. In some ways, it would have been easier for Paul to remain silent, but he knew so much was at stake, so he took a stand against them. Paul was an outsider. He wasn't like Peter. He didn't spend time with Jesus during his ministry years, but God was with him in that crucial moment.

In all these examples, there is a commonality. These people were not heroes. They were all characters in God's redemptive story. God was at work. He is still working. Something within each of these people stood firm. It was their inner convictions that they must do something. For them, action was imperative; it was their faith being lived out. We need courage to live out our own convictions. We will find ourselves with lions ready to tear us apart. God doesn't always stop the lions. He is always with us. God rescues and he saves.

You need to evaluate your family and your influence in this age. In some ways, church-orientated people think they are living in "Jerusalem," but more than likely, we are living in an age resembling Babylon. In Australia, most Christian people are unaware that, in this century, our country has departed from our once-held place in society. The neighbors are not interested in what we think. God is not a priority for them. Our moral views are not shared by everyone. We have become a nation that is not only confused with "big" issues and the like, but we have also adapted to our environment. It's no longer a conservative paradigm. Even Christian people have moved. People are evaluating their lives differently. Church is optional in many people's thoughts and practices. It may never have been a requirement for many. It's not a matter of returning to "Jerusalem" as much as it is a need to dig deep into our convictions with courage.

God is on a mission. Even in the church there are competing agendas supported by people who think their quest is crucial. We need to remind ourselves that we need to have a great deal of gratefulness in our hearts. God has rescued us. We have been redeemed. When we come together to sing worship songs, it must not be with our agendas in mind. They don't help us. We will always have to live among competing agendas. What our hearts need is an opportunity to pour praise out to our King. We need this. He doesn't need a boost. We need a heart for God, not a different agenda. In Daniels' story, there were competing agendas. In churches, there are always competing agendas. That is where conflict comes from.

Prior to the Babylonian exile, the prophet Jeremiah predicted that the Southern Kingdom, including Jerusalem, was going to be taken into exile for seventy years. People ridiculed him. His was a lonely voice. They answered that nothing bad was going to happen to them. Those predictions from Jerimiah proved to be true. Many of the Jewish people tried follow their traditions as they lived out their lives in Babylon. They grew comfortable in Babylon and never returned to Jerusalem. Their traditions didn't save them. The people in Babylon created new agendas. They fit into Babylon and never returned to Jerusalem. Their children grew up in Babylon. Generations lived without convictions. They grew uninterested in being rescued or saved. The culture of Babylon became their own.

Some people were repatriated to Jerusalem. Jerusalem was rebuilt. It was hard work. I have a challenge for your thinking: What do you offer your own nation? I'm convinced that small neighborhood churches have a purpose for the future. Typically, what happens is that traditionalism kills them. Often people seventy years of age and older determine the mission of the church. This should never be. The life of a church is displayed through current testimonies of what God has done in someone's life. If people are not being rescued and saved, it is because the church is out of sync with God. Oh, they may have well-worn traditions, but they are more than likely worn-out people who have long since settled in "Babylon." You need to take part in repatriation.

In my estimation, our current culture resembles Babylon. It is constantly changing, but never going anywhere. You should seize your "Miriam moments" and suggest what you are willing to contribute. Stop waiting for God to revive churches. Start working on how the gospel has seized you. You might be scared like Gideon and wish to dodge the battles. You might be having multiple conversations with God and lay all sorts of tests out for him. Quit. Have a meal with your friends. Talk about what God has placed in your heart. You know he has. You might think there is nothing you can do. Every age group is required, but traditions must not determine the direction of the church. Too many church meetings have too many uninterested traditionalists. We need a revolution of energized people showing a genuine interest in the mission life of the local churches. I don't mean sending money to foreign mission organizations or individuals even though that is important. I'm talking about you and your friends getting to work on something that results in lives being redeemed by God.

It's a together mission. God doesn't abandon churches, people do. Your convictions need to matter. In the same way that Anne went on the Ebola mission, you too can offer yourself. You might wonder what you will get out of serving God. I don't know that you will get anything. We need those same convictions. The neighbors around your church are more than likely uninterested in your church. Usually the culture around a church has moved on, and the people in the church think in terms of how to reach them. The truth is that people in the church don't even know how to reach their own families. Even a very small church can be potent by starting with the truth.

We need courage to see ourselves through his outcomes. Think about Daniel. He honored God with his prayer life. He took a stand for his convictions, but it cost him the most agonizing night of his life. I wonder what went through Daniel's mind. Look at the work God did in the life of the king. The king was already impressed with Daniel. He admired Daniel. He saw God in Daniel's faith. You will never know what someone sees in your life. Others will spot uninterest and traditionalism. Neither of those will move anyone anywhere. Your convictions will show up. Darius believed that somehow God would keep Daniel safe, and he did. Do you realize that it is not up to you to save the world? You can't even save yourself. God saves. You live. Jesus is the savior of the world. He rescued you, and he saved you from your sin. It's never been about how good you are or how amazing you are; it's always been about the goodness of God—his grace, his mercy, his kindness, his love.

Everything you are going through in your life is happening for a reason and has a purpose. Your calling, sacrifice, waiting, tasks, relocation, and the rest—it all matters. The Holy Spirit is at work for you. You still need courage. You need the courage of God. He is with you every step of the way.

CHAPTER 11

CRISES

Every now and then you hear about an unexpected heroic event that has taken place. In November of 2010, Qantas flight 32 out of Singapore bound for Sydney suffered an uncontained engine failure. The passengers on board heard two loud explosions, and immediately everyone on board was petrified. While flying around the world has become an everyday sort of thing, it is mind boggling when you think about what takes place. Being able to travel in a giant manmade tube 40,000 feet above the ground is a wonder of aeronautical genius. While the precision involved in manufacturing the various vehicles is extraordinary and well monitored, chance indicates there will be occasional failures.

The aircraft was an Airbus A380. For four hours, the pilot and crew battled incredible odds to hold together an aircraft with three partially working engines and the looming threat of a crash. There was no precedent for anything similar having taken place anywhere in the world, so the pilot had no way of knowing how to take care of the problem. It was a first. The pilot was Captain Richard de Crespigny. After he managed to calm the fears of his crew members, he was able, with their help, to return the flight safely to Singapore. I learned that the pilot handed out his personal phone number to all the passengers in case they needed to contact him for anything. That fact struck me as quite amazing. He was a professional pilot going through the most challenging experience of his career, but above everything else, he cared for his passengers. He gave of himself to them.

We are on a journey. God, by his Spirit, is leading us, so we have commonality. Some of our stories will intersect with the stories of others. We have similarities and differences, but even when we are different from someone else, we might share a small similarity. The one observation that I'm writing about in this chapter is crisis. We will all experience crises in our lives.

In September and October 2018, there were earthquakes and a tsunami in Indonesia. The devastation was massive. Where homes once stood, only foundations existed. Forests were flattened, and livestock was swept away. And at last count, well over twelve hundred lives had been lost. One survivor told the story of returning to rebuild his home after first burying seven members of his family. Here in Australia, we have been inundated with droughts. The famines created by the lack of rainfall is piercing into the fabric of our society. Farmers are distraught. Some have resorted to suicide. It's a national crisis. This is a country known for extended dry periods; however, currently this is a monumental problem. Obviously, flying in a plane with a dysfunctional engine would be a crisis.

You will face different crises in your life. If you have never had a personal crisis, you can be sure that you will at some time in the future. Sometimes they come upon you when you least expect them to. You might go through a sickness like cancer. Maybe a death of a child. Or a house that burns down.

I'm very fortunate because I get to speak to a lot of people of different ages. You would think that children would not necessarily be susceptible to personal crises, but I've found that many issues can threaten a child's well-being. For example, personal appearance is important. Kids as young as ten wrestle with what they look like, and they are often affected by personal identity issues. Teenagers are pressured by thoughts of what they will become as adults. Some people might think these are not serious issues, but I have known teenagers who have taken their own lives. Teenagers are often paranoid with fear that is generated by unreasonable expectations of their parents. When I am leading crusades in India, one of the most common prayers I hear coming from young people are prayers that they will do well with their studies or will be favored to graduate to the next part of their education.

A thirty-year-old will struggle with the feeling that they have, suddenly, become old. Seriously! Midlife crisis is a common theme among people of that age. I find that people in their late thirties are truly concerned that they are not successful enough. It's almost as if forty is a magical number, and everything in life should have somehow come together by the time a person reaches that age. The fear is that they have failed to create the life for themselves that they thought would have unfolded. This problem has to do with achievements and what they have done (or not done) with their lives. Again, I know several young men who didn't make it through that phase because they took their own lives. You might never have had problems along the way, but everyone has different assumptions, and in their lives, they process problems differently from the way you process yours.

Take, for example, fifty-year-olds. Both men and women of this age go into crisis mode if they lose their jobs. Perhaps it's because society doesn't view older people as able to contribute as much as younger people. I'm not sure. It is extremely difficult for a woman with a professional background to bounce back into full-time, career-driven fields. That alone creates a crisis. Add a divorce into the mix, and the recipe for a severe emotional breakdown is almost certain to occur. Early sixty-year-olds fear the future without a steady income. They worry about how much money they will have in retirement. Looking at their superannuation can be daunting.

The drama of crises doesn't ever end. I find that people in their seventies begin to go through challenging health issues. They are not as healthy as they used to be. They need knee and hip replacements as arthritis takes hold. Eighty-year-olds are often worried about losing life. They may lose a partner. Losing a partner at this age is quite common and extremely difficult. Many of people's friends pass away in that decade. Ninety-year-olds have the next problem. They are often lonely. They have fewer friends. If they are single at that point, the crisis has compounding issues. Getting to be a hundred years old is a feat. The problem that seems to surface is worrying about how much longer they can possibly live, or even if they want to live much beyond a hundred.

We are all different. Crisis is something that we all share at different times. Remember the Qantas pilot, Captain de Crespigny? The way he processed his crises in the moment was remarkable. Of course, then he had to take leave of absence so he could heal from the post-traumatic stress that he struggled with. I have found that it is not just major catastrophes that tear people down. People can be undone with all sorts of issues.

Now, I'm bringing all these observations up because I have noticed that both Christians and non-Christians struggle with similar issues. I have studied reactions in different people. I'm not sure if that pilot is a Christian. Yes, he handled his situation well, but I don't think he was a Christian. Christians don't seem to handle problems with any great degree of difference from the way non-Christians handle them. We seem to be drawn into similar patterns when we handle crises. It may be that we do it well; however, it may be that we might not do it so well.

The number of people that I have lost in my life through suicide tells me that there are bigger things to consider than the insignificant things that we (Christians) focus on.

We believe that the book 1 John are the writings of an old man. He may be ninety. In the letter, he talks to his congregation in such a way that makes me think of the pilot. He addresses them as little children. He gives them his phone number, if you know what I mean. He is giving them his experience. You see, the region was going through a crisis in the first century AD. The people were being persecuted. Some so-called religious people were beginning to discount the deity of Christ. They were downplaying who Jesus was. They were saying he wasn't God. The writer of the letter is John the elder who was the apostle who walked with Jesus. He made sure to tell people about his intimate relationship with the Christ and that Jesus called him the beloved. He knew Jesus like a brother. He was with him from the beginning of his ministry right through until the ascension of Christ. He knew that Jesus was God on Earth as a man. He wasn't about to let the congregation struggle with their faith without putting forward a timely word about what was true.

Dear friends, let us love one another, for love comes from God. Everyone who loves has been born of God and knows God. Whoever does not love does not know God, because God is love. This is how God showed his love among us: he sent his one and only Son into the world that we might live through him. This is love: not that we loved God, but that he loved us and sent his Son as an atoning sacrifice for our sins. Dear friends, since God so loved us, we also ought to love one another. No one has ever seen God; but if we love one another, God lives in us and his love is made complete in us.

This is how we know that we live in him and he in us: he has given us of his Spirit. And we have seen and testify that the Father has sent his Son to be the Savior of the world. If anyone acknowledges that Jesus is the Son of God, God lives in them and they in God. And so we know and rely on the love God has for us.

God is love. Whoever lives in love lives in God, and God in them. This is how love is made complete among us so that we will have confidence on the day of judgment: in this world we are like Jesus. There is no fear in love. But perfect love drives out fear, because fear has to do with punishment. The one who fears is not made perfect in love. (1 John 4:7–18)

We should know what it is like to be in love. We are also probably familiar with what it is like to be out of love. In this world, we are like Jesus. This is what God is doing in our lives. The Spirit of God changes us daily to become more like Jesus. We change. Our outlook on life goes through shifts, and we begin to view things more like Jesus does. We don't remain the same. There is no fear in love. Perfect love drives out fear. So, with pure logic in mind, if we are processing a crisis fearfully, it's possible that we have a love issue. We are either loving our way through life or we are more concerned about consequences of failure.

The driver in our lives can be love, or it can be fear. Remember, fear has to do with punishment. It's too easy to get caught up feeling as if we are going to fail or fall apart. When we think like that, we operate from a punishment point of view. It's the fear of crashing in a crisis. We worry about retribution or consequences. We are concerned about how various scenarios are going to play out. Christians can react as poorly as anyone; in fact, I find that people without faith may even process a crisis well. Interestingly, we forget God is in us. God is love. This is hard. If we fear, we are not made perfect in love. There is an adjustment in our lives. If fear takes hold of us, it is because God is not leading us as we process our crises.

There will be times in your life where you are at the controls. You will hear "explosions." You will know something is going wrong. How do you process your situation?

I recently saw a sign at a shopping center that read, "No grumpy people." Seriously. My guess is that it was a bit of a joke, but maybe it wasn't. People can be so negative about everything that they just become grumpy; in fact, that is their general disposition. It made me think about a conversation I had a few days before I saw that sign. I was speaking with a telemarketer who phoned me from Telstra, a mobile phone supplier in Australia. He was trying to sort out my requirements. The problem is simple. When you talk with a phone provider, they threaten you because you feel that, no matter what you agree too, it's going to be more expensive than it needs to be. They have the upper hand. You have no way of knowing how badly you will fare. I sometimes don't operate out of love in these situations. I instantly resort to fear. Love gets abandoned the second the call arrives. In these situations, unless we have already formed a relationship with a case worker, we fear that we are not going to get what we want at the end of the conversation. I wonder if Telstra has a "grumpy person" tag on my file?

Jesus said, "No greater love is there than this, than one who would lay down their life for their friends" (John 15:13). This is a pivotal verse in John's gospel. The context specifically refers to Jesus dying on the cross, and we should recognize that God in Jesus is calling people his friends. God is becoming the dying servant to save his people. Jesus put their lives ahead of his own. His comfort was erased. He was the love at all-cost sacrifice. If we are becoming more like Jesus, we need to start thinking along the same lines. We may focus on the dying because we might get out of living through what hurts badly. Death is not the primary consideration. Love is what stands out.

Whatever flight you are on or crises you face, you have an opportunity to end it so that your friends can walk free. The cause of Christ leads us to give our lives away so that others may live. This is hard, but it changes everything because it moves the center away from ourselves and places it with people with whom we will do life.

The Spirit of Holiness—the Spirit of God—in us leads us to where he wants us to go. He leads us to love. That is what is ultra-important in our lives—that Gods' Spirit takes us to love. Not to hate. We can do that easily enough. To love—there will always be a shift within us to lead us to love.

A crisis in life is often a reorientation of what is important, those things that explode into your conscious reality. What may have seemed important is no longer important. When crisis comes, your health may be taken away from you. What do you want? You want to get better. You might lose your house, your friends, your finances, your job, or your spouse.

Immediately you become aware of much more that takes priority. Fear can be the driver, or love can sit in the drivers' seat. You can always tell how you are traveling by what comes out of your mouth. What you say flows from what is stored up in your heart. The crisis can be God's part in changing us. Am I going to remain calm and love my way through this? Or am I going to hate through this, meaning that fear will move me forward? That might be an oversimplification of our reality, but it is such an important conversation to have. Am I going to lay down my life for another? Will I put my friends' needs ahead of my needs? Our friends matter. Jesus modelled his view. Our neighbors will see Jesus through our love for one another. "A new commandment I give to you to love one another, and by this all men will know that you are my disciples by your love for one another" (John 13:34–35).

God in his incarnational (skin-on) ministry, in all his glory, came and touched people he didn't have to touch. Jesus was open and honest with his life. Our neighbors will see Jesus through our love for them. Even your children will see Jesus because of the way you interact with everyday people. Kids will see Jesus in their parents' love for each other. Are we operating in fear or love? Only crisis will speak clearly.

CHAPTER 12

SEASONS

I spent much of my childhood living on the Island of Papua New Guinea. Because PNG presses in on the equator, there are two distinct seasons in that country—the wet season and the dry season. Obviously, it rains all the time in the wet season, and it doesn't rain very much in the dry season. We learned to live with both. When I first moved to Arkansas in the United States, it was the summer season; I received an extremely hot welcome. I learned over the next fourteen years to expect four distinct seasons each year.

Here in Brisbane, Australia, we also have four seasons, but they are certainly less distinct than the Arkansas seasons. Paul the Apostle wrote to Timothy and told him to be prepared to do his work in season and out of season. It seems to me that there are distinct times during which people are receptive to God's influence in their lives; at other times they are much less so. And so it will be in your life.

Western countries revolve around the school calendar. Here in Australia, almost everything in the life of the church tends to shut down during December and January. Perhaps it's because it is the middle of summer and hot, but I suspect people switch off in their minds and go into holiday season because schools close. Seasons are important. It's important to see the ebb and flow of community life during various seasons.

In Australia, much as it is in America, there are distinct seasons for various sports. Our rugby season begins in fall (autumn) and ends in spring. People almost don't know what to do when they are in-between sporting seasons. In November (late spring), Australia crawls into action with tennis. It's a big deal here. In Brisbane we kick off the season with tournaments, and then every other state follows along until we finally end up in Melbourne (January, midsummer) with the world-famous Australian Open.

In some ways, my role as a pastor is to be a spiritual coach, and so I take notice of all sorts of coaching scenarios. I'm often glued to the TV when the Australian Open rolls around. I have learned over the years to spot distinct differences between amateur players and the world-class professionals on the world tour. The commentators (ex-players and coaches) are always talking between the points when the players are working their way through the match, and the commentary is predictable. If a player is struggling in the match, invariably they begin to analyze the way a player serves the ball.

Amateurs who have taught themselves how to play usually have a rushed action. They get by with what they do, and nobody really worries too much about how they are serving so long as they manage to get the ball into the serving area. Professionals who play in the Australian Open are totally different. They make a living doing what they do, and they have well-honed skills. Their actions are distinct. The players seem to have developed series of movements that are well-developed intentional habits. A player might bounce the ball four times or tug on something, like a hat or shorts. The actions themselves aren't all that important, but they are usually consistent. Then it comes to the serve. A player might rock back and forth on his or her feet. When the time comes to throw the ball up, it usually goes to the same spot every time. Both arms work together in some sort of unified action. The ball-toss hand and the racquet hand are perfectly in tune. The racquet head strikes the ball, and the whole of the player's body follows in behind the ball. Amateurs usually achieve lower ball tosses, and they fall away from the follow-through. However, you can tell an amateur who has been well coached because he or she develops patterns that are like professional players' patterns. The actions are not based on talent as much as they are on a taught and highly developed skill. A person doesn't accidentally pick up these skills.

If a tennis club hires a tennis professional to work at the club, that "pro" has the job of improving the tennis playing at the club. While there are different grades of players, a seasoned veteran player might come to the coach for lessons. The coach wants to help that player. However, he or she is fully aware that it's hard to change every habit that a self-taught player has developed. There could be awkward times ahead. What the coach usually does is help the player focus on several new ways of thinking about one aspect of the game. Often the coach wants the player to improve the way he or she serves. The coach might change a grip on the racquet, or focus on the ball toss, or the follow-through. What the coach knows is that everything about that player can't be changed. The coach may be able to tweak only a bit of the player's game. We've all heard that it's very hard to teach an old dog new tricks. But children are different. They may not have the game or the power of an adult, but a coach can teach a child a more professional approach to his or her game right from the outset of the tennis experience.

Jesus was coaching adults. Sure, children were present in his illustrations, but Jesus was dealing with grownups. Grownups already have their way of doing life. Jesus had the task of slowly reorientating adults. He told them that, unless they became like little children, they couldn't receive the kingdom of God. There was no point beating around the bush. They had to change their entire perspective on life before they could grasp what Jesus was offering them. They had to be willing to trust where Jesus would lead them.

As a spiritual coach, I want to tweak your game by giving you a new way of looking at how you live your life. Rather than continuing to serve God through the same habits, I would like you to consider your spiritual life led by the Holy Spirit in a fresh and extremely memorable way. Let's face it, we would all like to serve with more impact. Too often we pick up habits that cause us to fall out of our serve, or we neglect the follow-through.

If you are being led by the Spirit of God, he will influence you toward holiness. God in his majestic ways declares you as holy and is making you holy. The book of Hebrews tells us that, without holiness, no one will see God (Hebrews 12:14). God is invisible. God is Spirit. However, he can be seen through holiness in faith. Jesus said, "Blessed are the pure in heart, for they will see God" (Matthew 5:8). God intends for us one day to see him face to face. As a believer in Christ, those who have trusted Jesus for their salvation have been declared perfect and justified. And so, the sacrifice of Jesus is what puts you in the right standing. Jesus promised you that he would be with you even unto the end. His promise is true. However, you can't see Jesus and so you can't see God. God sent his Spirit as a personal guide and teacher for believers. He is guiding us into his way of holiness. He leads, and we follow through with his way of doing life. We can be fairly awkward in how we serve him. The key is a willing compliance and desire to obey God because of his promises.

The Holy Spirit can be likened to a wind. You don't know the origins or destination of a wind, but you can recognize movement. You can tell when the wind is coming from a fresh direction and when it is more intense. Consider that God works in your life in distinctly different ways. So that you remember this converging principle, I'm going to liken the movements to the four seasons. We can all remember seasons. My idea isn't stated in scripture with the breakdown that I describe, but it is biblically derived. I can't change your life. I'm not trying to. I want to give you a new grip on understanding how to serve during distinctly different seasons. It's up to you what you do with this concept. It helps me to handle my game with more consistency.

Winter

Think of a bear in hibernation. It's fully alive but not active. How many times do Christians find themselves stepping back from active service? If you have spent any time in active church program service, you will also recognize the need to rest (not that I'm suggesting you compare yourself with a bear!). But the bear is designed by God to live through different seasons. Inactivity isn't the same as work avoidance. All I'm saying is that rest is necessary. When you sleep at night, you are rejuvenated. If you have sleepless nights, there is no way that you are able to be at your best. You need restful nights; you don't want to wake up like a bear with a sore head. Cranky Christians are no fun to be around. You are no exception. Think about time away from active church and active Christian service as an investment for a future season. Jesus said, "Come to me, all you who are weary and burdened, and I will give you rest" (Matthew 11:28). He also said, "I will pray the Father, and he shall give you another Comforter, that he may abide with you forever" (John 14:16 KJV).

The winter season of the Holy Spirit is recognized through your inactivity because God is repairing you. My picture is one of snuggling up on a winter's day with nothing planned. I like the idea of chopping wood, lighting a fire, and sitting next to a fireplace enjoying the family God has given you.

Spring

Think of new plants popping through the soil for the first time. I remember seeing tulips spring up from dormant bulbs planted well below the surface. This is the exciting season in your life when new plans have emerged or you are enthusiastic about worship in church. You don't have to force yourself to attend. You genuinely feel good about what you are doing. There's a spring in your step and an added kick in the way you serve. "Put on a new nature and be renewed as you learn to know your creator and become like him" (Colossians 3:10).

This is the season to develop new habits. If you are excited about Jesus and his new life, you should capitalize on your enthusiasm by reading his word. Try memorizing scripture. This is the perfect season to learn new verses. Look at how Jesus interacted with outsiders such as the Samaritan woman and do the same. Talk to people about meaningful things in their lives. Use this season for what it is. Operate your life with two motions going together. Speak truth through grace. Grace starts with forgiveness. Usually you have gone through humbling moments in preceding seasons, and pride isn't driving your conversations as much as the peace and joy through the power of the Holy Spirit. God will use the truth that you bring in love. Spring is marked by enthusiasm and grace-filled creativity.

Summer

Summer here in Australia means going to the beach and having a good time. However, that is not the picture that I have in my mind. I think of Arkansas in the summer. The first summer that I arrived there, it was scorching hot. I was working on a series of highway billboards in rural fields and feeling the drain of the never-ending sun. My example would have to be a visualization of slaves working in the cotton fields. It was an awful job. The people were abused and miserable. While slavery was abolished long ago, I've seen the fields. Somehow, those slaves experienced something most people have no clue about. God didn't cause the slavery; however, he did enrich the spiritual lives of those slaves. You only have to listen to the spiritual hymns and songs that came out of those regions to recognize that they experienced holiness, something slave owners knew nothing about. It's in the hardships of life that God produces a holy harvest. Sometimes you will find, through no fault of your own, sinful conditions forced upon you by people who are not much shy of being wicked. God will be with you in the worst times. Cry out to him. In your misery, lean into his grace because he has plenty to offer. Summer is a season in which you must keep going even though the days are excruciatingly painful. God will do a lasting work in your life.

The summer can also be self-imposed misery. The Spirit of Holiness can be pressing in on what needs to be changed in your life. Whatever sinful behaviors you have could be his objective. The Holy Spirit is responsible for converting you from unbelief to belief, and he does this through conviction of sin. He doesn't work to condemn you. He makes you aware of what is wrong. We tend to resist his work, which prolongs the hardship. God is patient. He desires that all will come to repentance, but God doesn't force your will. He can help you, but somewhere you must come to your senses and realize that you are in the wrong. This is hard to admit. Pride justifies you, or God justifies you. Not both. You can convince yourself that you are right with God, or God can convince you with his assurance through his saving work in your life. Hang in there; it gets better. You may well be regularly rebuked through God's word in this season. "No discipline seems pleasant at the time, but painful. Later on, however, it produces a harvest of righteousness and peace for those who have been trained by it" (Hebrews 12:11).

Fall

Fall, or autumn, is the preparing season. It is a season marked with shifts. If you travel to the northern Arkansas Ozarks in the fall, you will see the colors of leaves changing. What was green turns yellow, gold, orange, red, and maroon. It is an unbelievable scene, nothing short of spectacular. However, if you don't catch the picture in its full glory, you miss it because the leaves soon fall off the trees.

God is preparing you for what he has in mind. You will never remain the same person. The change could be quite profound. You will become what God wants you to become.

> So I say, live by the Spirit, and you will not gratify the desires of the flesh. For the flesh desires what is contrary to the Spirit, and the Spirit what is contrary to the flesh. They are in

conflict with each other, so that you are not to
do whatever you want. (Galatians 5:16,17)

We live with tension. It's as if there is a battle going on
between our will and God's will. The problem is that we
pretend that either side doesn't matter in big moments. But
they need to converge and work together. By nature, we are
not only independent, we have a rebellious spirit that loves to
be the boss in our lives and do whatever we think is best. You
don't lose who you are in the changes taking place, but you
learn to follow the inklings of what is best. God intends to
bring out the best in you. The way to do this is to learn how to
move with the rhythms of the Holy Spirit. That sounds easy,
but it's far from simple.

The best story for an example is one about King David.
David was supposed to be at war, leading his troops, but he
decided to neglect his position and stay in Jerusalem. Bathsheba
was married to Uriah the Hittite. He was away fighting, and
David decided to have a sexual relationship with Bathsheba.
She became pregnant, and David devised a scheme to hide the
fact and to also arrange for Uriah to die in battle. David then
took Bathsheba to his home as his wife. But he couldn't keep
his actions hidden from God. God sent the prophet Nathan to
inform David that he had done wrong. David was mortified,
but he did confess wrongdoing, and then he set about working
through forgiveness.

In a psalm, David penned the words, "Take not your Holy
Spirit from me" (Psalm 51:11 ESV). David was known as a
man after God's own heart, and he went through this "fallen"
season. David blew it. He knew he had. He was miserable for
the time between the moment he decided not to go to war
and the moment Nathan resolved his dilemma. The way I see

it, David loved God, but he allowed the flesh to dominate his sense of being holy, meaning set apart for God as the king. I think this story is necessary to help us learn that King David was awesome, but not above being a sinful man.

The fall season in our lives is one of preparing. God drew David into deep reflection through an encounter with the prophet. David could have ignored Nathan, but he chose not to. The season of reflection causes us to look at our lives and admit the truth about where we have failed. There is no condemnation for those who are in Christ, but there certainly will be confrontation about our intentional sinful life styles. God doesn't overlook us. His Holy Spirit convicts us in such a way that we will know we need help. Any prideful pursuit that has set itself up in our activities must fall away from our lives. God will love us through the process, but you will know holiness is the goal rather than fleshly pursuits.

The Seasons of our Lives Converge

Paul, the Apostle of Jesus, told Timothy to preach the word in season and out of season. He knew that there would be times when people were receptive to what Timothy preached and times when they would not. This is developed from Jesus's ideas of the soil in the heart. There are times when we listen and want to take in what God is saying and times when we do not.

In the Old Testament, we read about a prophet called Jeremiah. Not too many people listened to old Jerimiah; he was not a very popular preacher. He was God's man, but the nation of Israel didn't care too much for what he was on about. God told Jeremiah that he was going to give him a word for the people (Jeremiah 18). He told him to go to a potter's house, and from there he would get his message. When Jeremiah got to the potter's house, he watched the potter work.

I'm not sure if you have ever watched a potter prepare clay, but in India it's quite a scene. After the clay is dug up, the potter pours water on it and thoroughly mixes the water into the clay by stomping up and down on it with his bare feet until the clay is ready to be worked. Only then does the potter put a lump of clay onto the wheel where he will carefully shape it.

Jeremiah watched the potter begin to make a pot. The pot didn't take the shape the way the potter wanted it to; in the forming process it became marred. However, the potter didn't break it down or throw it away; rather, he skillfully reshaped it into what he saw it could become. It was in that demonstration that God spoke to Jeremiah about Israel. Israel hadn't turned out the way God intended, but God didn't discard the Israelites. Instead, he reshaped them during the seasons of exile.

God takes the raw material of our lives and pours into us what he knows we need. Then he carefully puts us on his sacrificial table of holiness. His hands skillfully shape us into what he intends to make of us. Sin disfigures us. He doesn't throw us away. He sacrifices himself as he makes us right. Carefully, hands on, he makes us into not only a new creation, but also into a useable vessel set apart for his devout purposes. The seasons of our lives converge to bring out what he intends to bring out.

CHAPTER 13

WRAP-UP

Jesus brought a whole new era into being with his life on Earth. He taught his disciples many things, but in my opinion, it was his connection to the Father that enabled him to complete his purpose. He taught his disciples how to pray. He taught them dependence on God. At his physical departure, he promised them that he would send them his Spirit. It is with the person of God, the Holy Spirit, that we live out our purpose on Earth. This book, *Convergence*, is about our Spirit-led journey.

The scripture that drove my thoughts as I developed this book is Romans 8:28: "In all things God works for the good of those who love him, who have been called according to his purpose."

Convergence is based upon a sermon series, a series that has been one of the most well-received aspects of my ministry. I have touched on twelve observations of Christian life that seem to be quite common. I likened it to twelve streams of thought that flow into a river of understanding. I don't think it is easy to retain a wholistic perspective on our lives, but much like the majestic display of the aurora, God's handiwork should be viewed with awe and wonder.

Your calling is foundational; it is God coming for you through his glorious gospel message. The element of sacrifice is important because God calls you to follow him, and to answer means giving up what is important to you. The principle of submission is hard to endure. No one likes to submit, but we learn that we receive extraordinary relational benefits through submission. God provides salvation completely, so our spirits soar when we learn of his provision. Perhaps one of the most challenging aspects of salvation is waiting. Being patient is important in our lives, and God makes us wait for our own good. God has good works in mind for us to do. It is in these tasks that meaning and purpose surface and we discover more of God's plan for our lives. With the tasks ahead of us, training prepares us for the good works that God has prepared for us. It's very interesting to see some developments in our lives and the way we take an interest in being trained. Being relocated is more common than we realize; however, its impact is massive in our Spirit-led journey. It's easy to overlook the resources that we have been blessed with. A great deal of courage is required, and it is available through God's work in our lives. The topic of crises raises all sorts of questions and concerns, but God seems to maximize our interaction with him during crises. The final observation considers the seasons of the Holy Spirit. It is an interesting look at a complex topic, but taking a different look at the Spirit's influence in our lives at different times should generate interesting conversations and a great deal of self-evaluation.

I trust that you have grown closer to God through the various considerations in this book and that you will be encouraged as you are led through life by his Holy Spirit.

ABOUT THE AUTHOR

L et's face it, we all want to be inspired. Writer, John Moore knows just how to inspire us to live a life that leaves the world better. John uses his experiences and biblical applications to help us understand the work of the divine in our lives. He easily finds intersections into the lives of a variety of individuals.

He has a gift. Over the years, God has enabled John to travel into new cultures and quickly grasp the essence of what is important to different people groups and generations. These experiences helped shaped John's view of the world, his work and the work of the divine. John's theological credentials include a Bachelor of Ministry and a Master of Ministry through Malyon Theological College and the Australian College of Theology.

Printed by BoD™in Norderstedt, Germany